GRANDPARENTS MAKE GRAND PARTNERS

How to Have an Eternal Impact on Your Grandchild's Life

LORI WILDENBERG

Published by D6 Family Ministry

ISBN: 9781614842026

WHAT GRANDPARENTS AND MINISTRY LEADERS ARE SAYING ABOUT THIS BOOK

There are so many amazing adjectives that apply to Lori Wildenberg's book on grandparenting that it's difficult to choose only a few. Not only has Lori written a thoroughly biblical book, but it may be the most practical book on Christian grandparenting today. It will help you navigate the nitty-gritty reality of life with your family in a manner that balances grace and truth. I know Lori personally and she is a godly grandparent who loves Jesus and is actively helping her grandchildren love Jesus. She doesn't just talk the talk; she walks the walk. She is a faithful guide to help you do the same with your grandchildren! This book is fantastic, and I cannot recommend it highly enough.

Josh Mulvihill, PhD
Author of *The Grandparenting Matters* book series

My friend Lori Wildenberg has had a ton of experience encouraging and coaching families. That fact is so evident in her latest book, *Grandparents Make Grand Partners*. It is super-loaded with illustrations, scriptural principles, and practical advice; so much so that I found myself chuckling one minute and choking up the next but more importantly, learning from Lori's wisdom. There's something in this book for every grandparent: all who read it will find plenty of places where they will think, "That's me!" *Grandparents Make Grand Partners* is easy reading and fast-paced, plus, the reflection questions at the end of each chapter make it a great tool for learning for individuals, small groups, or classes in churches. I'm thrilled to see this book added to the growing library of resources for Christian grandparents. It has my full endorsement!

Larry Fowler
Founder, Legacy Coalition

Most grandparents begin this season of life with high expectations. Lori's ideas and instruction will help them come true. Understanding the grandparent personalities will help you see how you come across, why you may be struggling, and what to do. They're significant! The blessings, benedictions, beatitudes, and promises are game-changers. They will provide you and your grands with peace and hope. If you're confused, you'll find answers in these pages, if you're angry—peace, disappointed—comfort, abandoned—compassion, and alarmed—solutions. The suggested prayers will enhance your ability to be an intentional Christian grandparent and that changes everything. Read and use the ideas here!

Dr. Kathy Koch
Founder of Celebrate Kids, Inc., speaker, podcaster, and author of eight parenting books including *Parent Differently* and *8 Great Smarts*

In a world desperately in need of godly generational wisdom and stability, *Grandparents Make Grand Partners* is a timely and tender guide for grandparents who long to pass down more than just heirlooms to their children and grandchildren. Lori Wildenberg beautifully captures the sacred role of grandparents as spiritual anchors, weaving Scripture, personal stories, and practical insights into a powerful call to eternal impact. This book is a must-read for every grandparent who wants to leave footprints of faith for generations to follow.

Heidi St. John
Author of *Becoming MomStrong: How to Fight With All That's In You for Your Family and Your Faith*, speaker, and host of the *Heidi St. John Podcast*

In *Grandparents Make Grand Partners*, Lori Wildenberg celebrates our God-given role as grandparents with a road map to navigate every phase of a grandparenting journey. Her warmth and wisdom provide encouragement for understanding the differing needs of each grandchild. With insightful information she covers everything from being intentional with daily and holiday rhythms to addressing complex family dynamics, from standing on biblical truths to using prayer to build bridges and strengthen bonds. This book is a treasure trove every grandparent needs.

Michelle Watson Canfield, Ph.D., LPC
Author of *Let's Talk: Conversation Starters for Dads and Daughters* and podcast host of *The Dad Whisperer*

Ken Canfield, Ph.D.
Author of *The H.E.A.R.T of Grandparenting* and president of GrandkidsMatter.org

As a passionate advocate for the profound intergenerational influence of grandparents, I wholeheartedly embrace this ministry, especially with the joy of having 15 grandchildren. It is both an honor and a privilege to be invited into their lives, guiding and nurturing them with love. However, with this honor comes the important responsibility to respect the boundaries set by our adult children. You might wonder how to navigate this delicate balance. That's where Lori's invaluable insights come into play. *Grandparents Make Grand Partners* offers practical, actionable strategies that empower grandparents to make a positive impact in their grandchildren's lives. Lori emphasizes the importance of leading with love, respect, and humility. By adopting the principles in this book, you can become the welcoming influence your grandchildren need. Let's embrace this incredible opportunity to connect deeply with the younger generation while honoring the family dynamics in place.

Rhonda Stoppe
Grandmother of 15, podcast host of *Old Ladies Know Stuff,* speaker, and author of seven bestselling books including, *Moms of the Bible: Life Changing Lessons From the Fearless, Flawed, and Faithful*

Lori is profoundly correct when she reminds us that if we only "want our grandkids to be happy," we have set a pretty low bar for ourselves and our family. There is much more to grandparenting than making kids happy. Lori offers practical and biblical perspectives for being more than just "happy-centric" grandparents. You will find the tools in this book that are not only instructive but convicting. If you want to be a grand grandparent, this is a tool you will want in your grandparenting toolbox.

Cavin T. Harper
Founder/president emeritus of
Christian Grandparenting Network

Grandparents Make Grand Partners by Lori Wildenberg is such a thoughtful and timely read. It's rooted in Scripture, full of practical wisdom, and speaks right to the heart of what it means to be a grandparent with purpose. I especially appreciated the reflection questions. They gently invite you to pause, think, and grow. This book lays out clear roles and responsibilities in a way that's encouraging, not overwhelming. If you're longing to build a meaningful legacy with your grandchildren, this book will bless and guide you every step of the way.

Connie Albers
Author of *Parenting Beyond the Rules,* founder of the
Equipped To Be with Connie Albers podcast,
speaker, TV and media contributor

When you become a grandparent, it's like getting an encore season of nurturing, loving, leading, and influencing. Different from parenting, it's an opportunity to continue to build your legacy in a new way. This book is chock full of wisdom for grandparenting in today's complicated world. If you're a grandparent, you need this book.

Jill Savage
Author of *Empty Nest, Full Life* and
host of the *No More Perfect Podcast*

I am a new grandfather. Sadly, when I was growing up, I only knew one grandparent, my grandmother, who had issues with alcohol. Needless to say, I want my grandchildren to experience something far better than I received. Lori's important book gave me a biblical game plan for how to connect with my grandchildren and point them to Jesus!

Dr. Rob Rienow
Founder of Visionary Family Ministries,
www.VisionaryFam.com

Grandparenting is easier than parenting because you get to bring the grandkids back home after outings! Yet in this age of smartphones and strained relationships with adult kids, grandparenting can come with unexpected challenges. This book will help you navigate your family dynamics with wisdom and grace. Lori Wildenberg puts the "grand" back into grandparenting.

Arlene Pellicane
Host of *The Happy Home* podcast and
author of *Grandparenting Screen Kids*

Today's grandparents face unique challenges in passing down their faith in an increasingly secular society. Lori Wildenberg's book is an essential tool for those committed to becoming an intentional, loving grandparent. She blends scriptural foundations and practical real-life applications to empower grandparents to cultivate deep spiritual roots that will last a lifetime in their grandchildren's hearts.

Lee Ann Mancini
Author of *Raising Kids to Follow Christ,* founder of
Raising Christian Kids, adjunct professor at
South Florida Bible College & Theological Seminary,
and executive producer of *Sea Kids*

This book is a treasure trove for Christian grandparents who want to make an eternal impact. I wholeheartedly recommend this inspiring and timely resource.

Dr. Scott Turansky
National Center for Biblical Parenting

Grandparents Make Grand Partners is a spiritually rich guide for every grandparent who longs to leave a lasting legacy of faith in the hearts of their grandchildren. With heartfelt stories, biblical wisdom, and practical tools, Lori Wildenberg encourages and equips grandparents to step into their God-given role with confidence and grace.

Ginger Hubbard
Bestselling author of *Don't Make Me Count to Three* and *I Can't Believe You Just Said That,* co-host of the *Parenting with Ginger Hubbard* podcast

Grandparents Make Grand Partners is a gracious, hope-filled, and honest book about a grandparent's role in helping children thrive. While looking through the lens of grandparenting styles, Lori provides helpful tips without becoming prescriptive, recognizing grandparents as a supportive, but crucial role in a child's life. I'm not a grandparent (yet) but found this book fascinating, and know this book will become a great conversation starter within families.

Christie Thomas
Award-winning author of books for families, including *Little Habits, Big Faith: How Simple Practices Help Your Family Grow in Jesus*

This book will open your eyes to the incredible opportunity you have as a grandparent—helping your grandchildren grow into happy, well-rounded children with a heart for Jesus and their eyes fixed on eternity. You'll discover how to move beyond making memories, to making disciples, as you learn practical and meaningful ways to impact generations to come by passing on a legacy of faith that will last into eternity.

Alyssa Seed
Founder and executive director of
Eternity Changers, eternitychangers.com

A thoughtful approach for grandparents, whether grands are being brought up with faith or not, with some ideas to help the parents of prodigals to pray and step gently. The book starts with encouraging grandparents to respect the parenting choices of their children. Practical tips and fun ideas to be intentional, weave in interaction with the three generations, and the prayers and role modeling of the grandparents provide opportunities to make a lasting impact on the grands.

Karen Whiting
Author, international speaker, creative, and grandma
who writes and lives to help families thrive

Lori Wildenberg knows how to knit hearts! I highly recommend *Grandparents Make Grand Partners* to draw relationships closer and imprint a lasting legacy for your family.

Pam Farrel
Author of over 60 books including bestselling *Men Are Like Waffles, Women Are Like Spaghetti,* co-director of Love-Wise.com

Grandparents Make Grand Partners is designed to navigate the joys and unique challenges of grandparenting. Mimi, as Lori's grands affectionately call her, has woven her experience as a mom, grandma, educator, and parent coach into this book. If you desire to create lasting, Christ-centered relationships with your grandchildren, *Grandparents Make Grand Partner* is a must read.

Becky Danielson, M.Ed.
Parent & family educator, speaker, coauthor of *Faithful Grandparenting: Practical Ideas for Connecting the Generations*

DEDICATION

This book is dedicated to the Papa
who loves and lives with this Mimi.

I love doing life with you. Sharing our love for
our grands is one of my greatest joys.

I love you,

The Wife of Your Life

ACKNOWLEDGMENTS

This book has been a joy to write. After being a guest on Legacy Coalition's Grand Monday Nights webinar, I have become passionate about being an intentional Christian grandparent. Many thanks to Larry Fowler and Barb Lorenz for lighting the fire!

Thank you to Ron Hunter, Danny Conn, and the team at D6 Family Ministry for believing in this project.

Dr. Kathy Koch, your belief in me and your gentle nudging continues to encourage me to step forward in faith. I am blessed to call you friend.

Robb Dunham, I am grateful for your wisdom and guidance.

Pastors James Hoxworth and Chuck Hess, you caught the vision for this project and provided the opportunity for my first grandparenting seminar at The Bridge Church. Thank you.

To my beta readers, fellow grandmoms, and friends: Maureen Behrens, Vicki Brock, Sandy Christianson, Mary Jacobs, and Lucille Zimmerman. Thank you for your prayers, time, talent, and love.

To my husband, Tom, thank you for your unwavering support and ever-present love. With an eye for detail, you read every word to make this book the best it can be. Also a big thanks for taking on dinner responsibilities so I could write.

With a full heart I want to thank my children along with their precious spouses. I am grateful to God that you share the desire to pass along faith to your children.

To my five grands, you are my inspiration. I am beyond blessed to be your Mimi.

Thank you, to my Heavenly Father, whose faithfulness and love endure through the generations.

CONTENTS

Introduction

The Grand Effect

"SOME OF OUR GREATEST BLESSINGS CALL US GRANDMA AND GRANDPA."

One piece of paper remained. It was neatly folded into a small square. The text inside supplied the answer to the game's question, "What do you look forward to as you get older?" The winner would be the one who came closest to my answer.

Game night at the cabin is a common occurrence. My kids, husband, mom, and additional family members were playing Best Guess at my mom's cabin in northern Minnesota. Some solid guesses from the players included: More time with friends, time to start and finish a book, sleep in as long as you want, take more vacations, no cooking, and go on more date nights. All ideas I could get behind, with the no cooking answer being especially appealing. I unfolded the last piece of paper and read, "Having grandkids." The no cooking answer moved to second place. Having grandkids was the best guess.

Even though I was certain I would love having grands, I couldn't picture being a grandmom. At the time, my kids were in fourth, seventh, eighth, and tenth grade. The grandparent role seemed a long way off. Having grandkids, well that was for older folks, that was for people my parents' age.

The wise and winning answer was supplied by my seventh-grade middle school daughter, Samantha. Fast forward to the present day, Samantha is now a mom and just had child number three. I have been a grandmom for six years. Samantha was right. Having grandchildren is something to look forward to, it is a blessing to embrace. What I did not realize, yet have come to understand, is that my Mimi role and my husband's role as Papa is a divine calling.

In Acts 16 we meet Lydia, a businesswoman, who had a divine calling. The Lord opened her heart to respond to the gospel message Paul preached. Not only was Lydia converted but God used her and her influence to impact her entire household. All those living under her roof were baptized along with Lydia. The Lord used her to reach the souls in her home. God can use us too, if we are willing.

Grand Stats

Before we get into our God-given calling, let's examine some statistics. It is interesting to note that most first time grandparents are not considered seniors but middle-aged, with middle age "generally defined as being between the ages of 40 and 60."[1] The average age of a first-time grandparent is fifty years for women and a couple years older for men.[2] In fact, one third of the adult population are grandparents, who have an average of five to six grandchildren.[3] Combine those statistics with the fact that grandparents are second only to parents in terms of a child's emotional and spiritual development, and we realize grandparents are a spiritual force. [4] Fellow G-Mas and G-Pas, GiGis and Poppys, ViVis and Bumpas, Gammys and Gampys, Mimis and Pappas, we have a bigger purpose than spoiling our grands. We have influence, great influence. God calls us to step up. Our relationship with our grandkids matters eternally. The Lord wants us to partner with Him. He beckons us, He commands us, to be a part of our grandchildren's spiritual formation and pass the baton of family faith. Scripture confirms this in Deuteronomy 4:9, "Only be careful, and watch yourselves closely so that you do not forget the things your eyes have seen or let them fade from your heart as long as you live. Teach them to your children and to their children after them."

Grand Benefits

When our son and daughter-in-love were expecting their first child—the one who made Tom, Papa, and me, Mimi—Jaime dangled a carrot, "Watching grandchildren strengthens a grandparent's mental and physical health." I really did not need to be persuaded. Watching my little grand one day a week for the first eighteen months of his life was an easy sell.

Our daughter-in-love was correct. Watching grandchildren has a positive effect on the grandparent's brain and body.[5] A study on aging done in 2016 showed that grandparents who babysat grandkids lived thirty-seven percent longer. Those who provided childcare were more physically fit and experienced less stress. [6] Time grandparents spend with their grandchildren improves mental sharpness and overall health.

On the flip side, grandparents positively impact the mental and emotional health of their grandchildren. Studies show children need four to six adults in their life for stability and emotional and social development.[7] An article in *Good Housekeeping*, points out the positive impact regular interaction between grandparents and grandkids has on the grandchildren's mental health.[8]

Culture Cues

Being an intentional Christian parent is countercultural. Throughout Scripture we see how God commands each generation to pass their faith and their faith experiences to the next generations. Our culture today does not value this. It speaks loudly about what this final third of our lives should look like.

We hear:

- You earned it.
- Buy it if you want it.
- Take a break.
- Take a cruise (Okay, I am all for this one if it is a River Cruise).
- Play pickleball.
- Move to a retirement community.

There is nothing wrong with any of these endeavors. But I have noticed a theme. As we move into retirement age, culture tells us, it is time to be a little selfish and receive our reward. But what if this time was more about being selfless? Being available and flexible? Again, none of these cultural experiences are wrong, but should they be our top pursuit? I wonder, is this a clever distraction by the enemy (the devil) so we do not live out our God-given calling to be the grandparents we are created to be?

Dr. Josh Mulvihill, in his book, *Discipling Your Grandchildren*, states, "Grandparents need to reject the narrative that the purpose of old age is a life of leisure and self-indulgence."[9] If our ultimate goal is to see our family in Heaven, we must make an effort to carve out time for our adult children and grandchildren to intentionally influence their faith.

Grand View

I like to think of our Mimi and Papa roles as a three-way partnership between us, with our grandkids' moms and dads, and with God.

The grandparent's hat is different from the parent's. We no longer call the shots. Our involvement is largely determined by our adult children.

Between these pages you will find loving plus easily applicable and practical ideas for interaction with your grands, gain new respect for your adult children's choices, and discover how to impact your grandkids' faith. You will identify which one of the nine different grandparent personalities best describes you, recognize unhealthy family patterns, move toward healthy godly design, appreciate generational differences, and examine why adult children may implement boundaries. You will discover ways to avoid or address common relationship misunderstandings or problems that occur between parents and grandparents. The grandparent and parent roles will be defined so the grandparent is able to respectfully embrace the shift from parent to grandparent. We will unpack the critical life-giving messages our adult children, in-laws, and grandchildren need to combat the cultural influences of identity and sexuality.

Through present day grandparent stories and past biblical accounts, we will examine the grandparent role and influence in the family. Practical ways to navigate heart-wrenching issues like mental health, physical distance, spiritual differences, faith deconstruction, and complicated or estranged relationships will be provided. We will humbly look at what to do about grandparent competition or jealousy. Fun ways to weave faith into holiday celebrations will be provided. Many of those who shared their heart and experiences with me (and now you) prefer to remain anonymous. To honor their request, I have changed their names and altered some details.

Your confidence in being a co-cultivator of your grandchild's faith will increase as you relate to the stories and implement the activities, conversations, prayers, and blessings. Partnering with our children, as they raise theirs, is good for all; good for our grandkids, good for our adult children, and good for us. It is an honor to be a participant with our Heavenly Father in our grandchildren's spiritual formation and unique calling.

Paul, in 1 Timothy 1:2, called Timothy his true son in faith. Timothy acted as Paul's representative in many churches and then pastored the church in Ephesus. In 2 Timothy 1:5, Paul mentioned Timothy's mother and grandmother. Both Eunice, Timothy's mom, and Lois, his grandmom, shaped Timothy's faith. "I am reminded of your sincere faith, which first lived in your grandmother Lois and in your mother Eunice and, I am persuaded, now lives in you also."

These two Jewish women partnered to prepare Timothy, even as a baby, to recognize the Messiah, "and how from infancy you have known the Holy Scriptures, which are able to make you wise for salvation through faith in Christ Jesus" (2 Timothy 3:15). Because of the teaching of his mom and grandmom, he was ready and able to receive the good news of the gospel and then later to be used by God to bring the good news to others.

We can be like Lois. Do not underestimate the impact our faith has on our grandchildren. The faith that lives in us can live in our grandkids, too. Let's partner with our children and with the Lord to ready the hearts of our grands to receive Christ and fulfill their unique purpose in God's kingdom.

Do not underestimate the impact our faith has on our grandchildren.

In this final third of my life, God has clarified what is most important. Time is fleeting. I want to invest my time in faith-building opportunities. Faith, my faith, my husband's faith, and my family's faith. Sure, having nice things is nice, taking exciting trips is exciting, and of course celebrating wins and accomplishments brings joy. But it all pales in comparison to my loved ones knowing, loving, and serving Jesus.

Most grandparents today consider themselves pretty good Grammys and Grampys. And they are most likely right. They are probably involved, loving, and caring. Yet as a Christian grandparent we realize there is more to it, isn't there? The stakes are high. The enemy is in a big battle for the souls of our grandkids. We must not get distracted or complacent.

I have heard the statement that comfort can be an idol. That's convicting. I like my comfort. I like a good night's sleep. I do not want to be too hot, too cold. There is even a name for this concept, The Goldilocks Principle where things are, "Just right."[10]

Let's not settle for just a Goldilocks comfortable and close relationship. Let's roll up our sleeves and co-cultivate faith in our grands with our Heavenly Father and our adult children. The grandparent bar must be raised from merely being a babysitter or fun playmate to a person who can impact our family member's eternity and kingdom calling.

Just think of it. We are one third of the population.[11] Grandparents have an average of five to six grandkids.[12] What a fierce faith-filled force we could be if we partnered with God to nurture faith in our grands. We have a God-given purpose, an eternal focus, to encourage our grands to embrace their faith in Jesus.

Cavin Harper states in his book, *Courageous Grandparenting: Unshakeable Faith in a Broken World*, "Successful grandparents know it is not just about the grandkids and them. I hope you recognize that our top priority is to figure out how parents and grandparents work together as allies, not adversaries. Our goal is to work together toward the same objective—to help our grandchildren become all that God wants them to be. Our job is to find ways to foster an environment in which our adult children can become the greatest parents possible."[13]

Being a good YaYa and PawPaw may encompass childcare, gift giving, fun times, laughter, and providing family history. These are all desirable things. Yet Scripture tells us our relationship with our grands has present impact and eternal implications. We can be a vital and integral source of support for our adult children's role as parents and for our grandkids' social and emotional development, mental health, and spiritual growth. Let's be willing and available to partner with our great God to intentionally draw our grandkids toward a saving faith in Jesus Christ.

I am fired up about being intentional in passing the torch of faith to my grandkids, just as Lydia was when she passed along her faith to her entire household. Do you feel the same? Rise up with me as we learn together how to connect and protect our faith and family through the blessing of grandkids. Purpose built on God's Word is the most powerful weapon against the enemy's schemes.

Perhaps this comes as no surprise to you, but as I am walking this grandparent journey, I have learned having grandkids is far better than no cooking—which, I have realized, will never be realized.

Since my youth, God, you have taught me, and to this day I declare your marvelous deeds. Even when I am old and gray, do not forsake me, my God, till I declare your power to the next generation, your mighty acts to all who are to come.

Psalm 71:17–18

Grand Reflection

1. When you were parenting, what did you picture this stage of life would look like?
2. Which statistic or perspective in this introduction, "The Grand Effect," impacted, encouraged, or surprised you?
3. How can you strengthen your own faith, so you are prepared to impact your grandchild's faith?

Grand Verses

Read, reflect, and respond to these verses:

- Acts 16:11–15
- Psalm 71:17–18
- 2 Timothy 1:5
- Deuteronomy 4:9

What do you learn from these passages?

Grand Partner Tips

- Strengthen your faith by reading God's Word each day.
- Each day, spend time in prayer talking with God about your grands.
- Even if your spouse is not on the same page, you can still be like Eunice in 2 Timothy 1:5 and impact your grandchild's spiritual development.

Grand Prayer

Heavenly Father,

Thank you for the gift of grandkids. Help me not to be complacent and comfortable in my interactions. Move me to intentionally and lovingly share my faith in You so my grandkids' hearts, minds, and souls desire to follow You. Amen.

Chapter 1

Grand Personality

"A GRANDPARENT IS A LITTLE BIT PARENT, A LITTLE BIT TEACHER, AND A LITTLE BIT BEST FRIEND."

"You are right," Amy, my sister-in-law exclaimed. "I think there are different grandparent personalities." We had been chatting about my idea for writing this book and the inclusion of grandparent personalities. I appreciated her confirmation.

Just as I noticed other parents' parenting styles before I became a parent, I have been paying attention to how grandparents, grandparent. I observed my neighbor who watched her eight-year-old grandson one day a week in the summer. I watched her interact with him and noticed the joy that exuded from both. Many days they would get on their bikes and go for an extended ride. I decided I wanted to be that type of grandmom, active and involved.

"Mom, I think you will be like Nana when you have grandkids," my eldest child, Courtney, declared. My mom never missed a special date. I want to be that type of grandmom too. My mom's philosophy is, "My job isn't to parent. My job is to love my grandkids." She has always been respectful of her kids' parenting styles and has loved her nine grandkids well.

Time, fun, and respect are all critical components of a healthy relationship. But what about weaving faith into the equation? I asked my daughter, Kendra, how her grandparents may have impacted her faith. "I knew church and church activities were important to all my grandparents. Reading Pops' poetry made me realize the depth of his faith. His poems made me want to feel the connection to God he felt. I could tell he knew God's character and had a personal relationship with Him. Pops' writings express that. It caused me to wonder what it would feel like to be able to write something like that. His poetry stirred curiosity in me and planted a seed, a ruminating thought."

My maternal grandmother, Gram, played games, supplied us with Cracker Jacks, occasionally babysat, and talked about her church participation. This seemed good too. My paternal Grandma would belt out the hymn, "What a Friend We have in Jesus," even when her body was weak and frail. Their approach was more indirect. Both of my grandmothers provided a subtle influence regarding faith.

The way in which we parented could affect the way in which we relate to our adult children and grandkids. This is something to be aware of. By reflecting on our past parenting style, "Was I more rules or relationship focused?" we will be cognizant of past patterns. There are grandparent pluses and pitfalls to either approach. If rules were the focus, order and obedience are highly valued. If a relationship takes the top position, fun and connection take top priority.

As we examine the different grandparenting styles, we realize no approach is perfect. Some ways are more desirable than others if we hope to partner with our adult kids and God, in the quest for our grandkids to know the Lord and grow into their God-given purpose. We will make note of the positives and potential negatives of each style.

Personality Plus

It appears to me there are nine main grandparent personalities. Like me, you will most likely find you are a blend of a few types. Let's determine your dominant grandparent personality. We will do this by seeing how you respond to this fictitious question posed by your grandchild. Keep in mind, this is a fun exercise, meant to raise our awareness of how we interact with our grands and how that may affect our adult children.

Your grandchild asks, "Can I have a cookie?"

You respond:

Sure, anything you want.	Chum
After dinner.	Captain
Let's ask your parents.	Consultant
May I have a cookie?	Ceremonial

If it's gluten, dairy, or sugar free.	Cool
(Decision maker, functions as parent while watching kids)	Surrogate
Let's ask your parents then let's say thank you to Jesus for the cookie.	Christian Coach
(Unavailable to ask, disengaged by choice)	Checked out
(Unavailable, blocked by parents)	Canceled

Which answer best describes your first response?

Now let's look at the pluses, pitfalls, and perspective challenge of each personality.

Chum: The Fun and Perhaps Favorite Grandparent

Plus Side: Builds a strong relationship with the grandchild. Often considered the fun grandparent.

Possible Pitfall: May have difficulty following the parents' rules and requests if they conflict with the child's desires or fun. Avoids difficult conversations for the sake of the relationship.

Probable Proclamation: "What happens at Grandma's stays at Grandma's."

Positive Adjustment: To support the parents even if the grandchild is unhappy.

Tom as Papa embraces grandparent playfulness. As a dad he fell more into the authoritative personality. But as Papa he is free from the day-to-day responsibility of raising a child and fully enjoys his time with the grands. The grandkids love it too. He's the guy who will laugh when he's soaked by the squirt gun or will stack the deck so he loses at a card game of War. Tom and I are learning not to laugh when the grands do something their parents are attempting to correct. It can be tough not to chuckle at some of the things the kids do. We see their behavior as delightful or perhaps a short-lived phase. Our adult kids feel undermined when we do this. They prefer we support their efforts to train their kiddos.

Captain: The Authoritarian Grandparent

Plus Side: Decisive. Orderly.

Possible Pitfall: Inflexible, stubborn.

Probable Proclamation: "My house, my rules."

Positive Adjustment: To increase connection and let go of control.

"My in-laws were very controlling and manipulative. They wanted my children to look and behave in a very specific way. They volunteered to watch my daughter while my husband and I went out on a date. I came back to my daughter sporting a new haircut. My first born got her first haircut without me, without my permission. My in-laws did not get to see me or my daughter for six months until they apologized. Their apology was more like a surrender. 'Fine. You win. We won't touch your kid again.' After that, our relationship was very tense."—Justine B.

Justine's story is a big warning for grandparents who are prone to call the shots. We must remember our grandkids are not our children. The more control we try to assert, the more boundaries their parents will likely impose. This will affect our relationship with our adult kids, their children, and our ability to be a faith-focused influencer.

Larry Fowler asserts that the more control grandparents attempt to exert the less influence they will have in their grandkids' lives.[14]

Consultant: The Grandparent Who Steps Back and Waits for the Parents to Weigh In

Plus Side: Supportive of the parents' rules and requests.

Possible Pitfall: Wishy-washy, maybe hesitant to act in matters that require immediate correction.

Probable Pondering: "Have I said too much, or too little?"

Positive Adjustment: To speak truth with grace if asked.

I recall a situation where one of my grands was a little disrespectful to another adult. I was surprised and even found the comment a tiny bit funny. I hesitated to address the disrespect. The parents were not around so I should have gently jumped in. I could have offered my grand an alternative respectful response. I asked my adult child if it would be okay in those situations for me to speak up. I was given the green light so going forward I will handle this type of situation differently.

Ceremonial: The Grandparent Who Values Good Manners and Family Traditions

Plus Side: Passes along traditions and family history.

Possible Pitfall: Difficult to see other's point of view.

Probable Proclamation: "We've always done it this way."

Positive Adjustment: To be flexible when it comes to holidays.

"My father-in-law valued tradition. Before we came to visit for an extended weekend, he declared, 'We are going to teach these kids some manners. Dinner is at 7:30 and everyone will sit at the table until we are all done.' In my opinion, my kids had decent manners for being so young. They were two, four, and five, 7:30 was way too late to feed them. I was offended at the implication that I had not taught my kids manners. To avoid conflict, we complied with the dinner time and sit-down rules but also gave our kids a hefty snack around 5:30. When my kids were little, visiting their home stressed me out. I wished my husband would have spoken up."—Laine A.

Laine's story shows how a ceremonial grandparent may miss the bigger picture. In this case the entire family came to visit. Making the visit pleasant is a higher priority than a late meal. Emphasizing ritual over connection gets in the way of faith building opportunities. Most grandparents don't share everyday meals with their grands. Prioritizing gratefulness for food and family, through prayer, would be a better tradition to zero in on. The parents can worry about manners.

Cool: The Grandparent Who Highly Values Cultural Trends, Mores, and Embraces a World Rather Than a Biblical View

Plus Side: Understands today's culture, may be relatable, current with trends and technology.

Possible Pitfall: May choose cultural relevancy over biblical truth.

Probable Proclamation: "Follow your heart."

Positive Adjustment: To choose biblical truth over cultural trends.

My cousin Karen and I aspired to be like my maternal (her paternal) grandmother. We considered "Gramma Herbert" our mod grandmother. Her clothes were up to date, she was adventurous and traveled with friends, knew all the Minnesota Vikings and Minnesota Twins stats, and was up for family games at the cabin with her grandkids. Our mod Grandma was a person we could relate to and have fun with. My interaction was different with Gramma Herbert than it was with my paternal grandparents.

Here's what Susie W. has to say, "My children's dad and his entire family, go so far as to try and make my Christian lifestyle look cultish to my children. And they use this to seek custody. It's not easy being the only Christians in the family."

Surrogate: The Grandparent Who Provides Regular Childcare but Does Not Have Full-Time Custody

Plus Side: Meets child's needs while supporting her adult child and their spouse.

Possible Pitfall: May take over or interfere in parents' decisions or discipline.

Probable Proclamation: "I'll take care of it."

Positive Adjustment: To let go of the reigns when the parents are around.

I have had temporary and short stints with this role. When my daughter had her babies, she asked me to come and help. I jumped at the chance. Once babies two and three arrived, my main two jobs were to make meals and watch the older kids. It is difficult not to enter the fray after caring for the kids all day. Today there are many grandparents who function as surrogates and watch their grandkids regularly. (A grandparent with full-time custody fully functions as a parent.)

Statistics show over half of those who provide childcare watch their grandkids under twelve hours a week. About twenty-four percent watch their grands twelve to twenty-five hours per week. And one in four grandparents care for their grandkids twenty-five or more hours a week.[15]

Christian Coach: The Grandparent Who Intentionally Encourages a Christian Worldview and Faith Development

Plus Side: Filters thoughts and feelings through intentional faith conversations and actions.

Possible Pitfall: May come across as pious, uses Christianeze, and speaks in platitudes.

Probable Pondering: "How can I show Jesus in this moment?"

Positive Adjustment: To be ready to respond authentically with humility and grace.

Diane Fowler is a great example of an intentional Christian grandparent. Her middle school grandson asked her if she would participate as a leader with him in a church event.[16] She could have said, "Been there, done that." But instead, she set aside whatever she could have been doing during that time frame and jumped in with both feet. She wants to encourage her grandson, their relationship, and his participation in church activities while hoping to simultaneously grow his faith. This was a spiritual win-win!

This approach, when stretched to its extreme, and this grandparent could be viewed as hypocritical. Real conversations come as platitudes are regularly spoken.

Checked Out: The Grandparent Whose Interests and Schedule Trump Everything Else

Plus Side: Grandparent is meeting his or her personal needs or wants.

Possible Pitfall: Uninvolved.

Probable Proclamation: "I already raised my kids."

Positive Adjustment: Get involved. Be a student of your grandkids. Get to know their likes and dislikes.

"My parents are uninvolved grandparents. No matter what we try, we can't get them involved in their grandkids' lives. They live 1,000 miles away. They see us once a year and it is like pulling teeth to get them to do much. They did come out for the girls' graduations. Even with my dad battling cancer, they have little interest beyond a passing conversation. They don't text, call, or engage on Facebook. Nothing. Christmas, they send money. My kids have always felt hurt that their grandparents aren't involved. In all fairness though, that was their parenting style."—Jenna B.

Reasons for lack of involvement may include grandparents who are still in the workforce, their energy level, medical issues, or just simply not wanting to babysit. An article in *Parents* magazine addresses the phenomenon of uninvolved grandparents. Part of what contributes to this is Boomers and Gen Xers are programmed to be busy. They work out, volunteer, are involved in various social clubs, and value going on trips. They are not interested in surrendering their time.[17]

Grandparents, we know time is a precious commodity. The older we get, the more we value time and cherish time with loved ones. We have a window of opportunity to impact our grandkids' lives, their mental health, emotional well-being, and spiritual growth. We can still do fun things and be more carefree. However, we must be cognizant of how we spend our time and realign our priorities according to the charge our good God has given grandparents.

Canceled: The Grandparent Who Is Estranged From Their Adult Children and Grandchildren, Not by Choice

Plus Side: Could be moved to address past wounds in order to reconcile.

Potential Pitfall: Heartbroken. Separated.

Probable Proclamation: "I'm not allowed to see my grandkids."

Positive Adjustment: Be a bridge builder. First work on your relationship with your adult child. Admit, "I can do better."

This situation is heartbreaking. Many parents who told me their stories are baffled as to why their adult children are so angry and want to keep them out of their lives. Some of those stories are included in Chapter 4, "The Grand Gap."

We must be cognizant of how we spend our time and realign our priorities according to the charge our good God has given grandparents.

Which type or types best describe you? What are you doing well? Where could you improve?

We have tendencies toward certain styles. Each tendency has the power to positively or negatively impact our adult children and grandkids. If you have caught the vision of being used by God to impact your grandchild's faith, being a Christian Coach must land in the primary personality category. A grandparent who is a Christian Coach guides, prays for, prays with, and encourages family faith, and will eternally impact the grandchildren's faith.

When the Christian coach is combined with the Chum, Captain, Consultant, Cool, Surrogate, or Ceremonial personality your grandchild's faith will be positively impacted. Of course, be aware of the possible pitfalls and make the necessary positive adjustments. Each personality, stretched to its extreme, has negative implications.

If you find yourself in the Checked-Out category yet realize you have a desire to pass along your faith, it's not too late. God can make up time in the air. Hopefully this informal exercise will raise your awareness and encourage you to realign your priorities. If you fall into the Canceled group, and wholeheartedly desire to be a Christian Coach, I pray you humbly seek the Lord and pursue healing your relationship with your adult children (this is discussed more in the upcoming chapters).

Our Adult Child's Impact

"I've been surprised at how much my adult children's view of my role has impacted the way I grandparent. I wasn't expecting that." Cindy P. expressed this frustration in a grandparenting class I was teaching after I posed the question, "What has surprised you the most about being a grandparent?"

The type of grandparent we are depends, to a large degree, on how our adult children see our role. Our adult children's view and their expectation of the grandparent role impacts how and how often we relate to and interact with the grandchildren. This may be different among your adult children, and it will affect the way in which you interact with grands from different families. Are you seen more as a playmate, a free babysitter, a holiday host, a fan in the stands? Or do they recognize that you are a vital source of support for them and for their children?

I've noticed I'm a slightly different grandparent to our different families who have kids. One family lives out of state. Another a few miles away. One family loves to have Tom and me take their kids for short excursions, the other family likes their entire family to be a part of any fun-filled activity. One family is more concerned about germs and illness, the other less. One family is more comfortable with planned events; the other is open to spontaneity. No way is right or wrong. These are just personal preferences, which may be different from the way we would do things. It is important to remember, these choices are a parent's call. As grandparents we need to keep in mind, it is more important to support our children's parenting decisions and efforts than to force our personal preference.

It is good to have fun, watch the kids, host events, and be a fan. Yet as grandparents we can be so much more. We can be a source of spiritual support for the grands. We are an untapped faith resource. Let's open that spiritual spigot.

Children's children are a crown to the aged,
and parents are the pride of their children.
Proverbs 17:6

Grand Reflection

1. Which three personalities do you display most often?
2. Which is your dominant personality?
3. What are some positives, negatives, and challenges you have seen or experienced? Where can you improve?

Grand Verses

Read, reflect, and respond to these verses:

- Proverbs 17:6
- Ephesians 6:1
- Ephesians 6:4
- Colossians 3:21

What do you learn from these passages?

Grand Partner Tips

- Be the Christian Coach who expresses and models faith in an authentic, relatable, and grace-filled way.
- Be the Chum and find engaging faith-filled ways to connect with your grands.

- As the Surrogate or Consultant, support and respect your children in their quest to be the best parents they can be.

Grand Prayer

Heavenly Father,

> Thank you for this opportunity to enjoy my grandchildren. Give me an awareness of the importance of time spent together and use me to support and respect my adult children so they can be the parents you have called them to be. Give me the words and creative ideas on how to encourage and cultivate faith in my grandchildren. Amen.

Chapter 2

Grand Family Dynamics

"REMEMBER AS FAR AS ANYONE KNOWS WE ARE A NICE, NORMAL FAMILY."

"Remember as far as anyone knows we are a nice, normal family." This statement is displayed on various types of home décor like decorative pillows, framed signs, and coffee mugs. Homer Simpson articulated this statement in the Simpson's TV show.[18] One of John Ortberg's book titles dovetails Homer's words perfectly, *Everybody's Normal Till You Get to Know Them.*[19]

Homer and Ortberg are spot on. Each family has their own type of normal, with a little disfunction mixed in. Not one family, not one person, is perfect.

In my coaching practice, most of my current clients have concerns or difficulties with their adult children. They desire to improve or even to simply have a relationship. There are many reasons why parents and adult children struggle or are estranged.

As we examine various ways family members relate, remember we can choose the best and most godly way to interact. We won't do life together perfectly and that is okay. As we read through Scripture, particularly the Old Testament, we see sinful people in imperfect families. In the middle of our mess, we find a God who restores and forgives even the most dysfunctional of families. In the process of our *unnormalness* we have an opportunity to grow. God teaches us humility, repentance, and unconditional love. These are three main ingredients to the connection concoction.

Levels of Connection

How connected are you to your adult child and their spouse? Your relationship, either healthy or unhealthy, with your adult children will impact your connection to your grandkids.

Toxic relationships have a high degree of negative connection. They are often characterized by negativity, criticism, control, selfishness, disrespect, competition, insecurity, blame, jealousy, or even abuse. The receiver of these poisonous patterns may display low self-esteem, anger, guilt, or shame. (In an upcoming chapter we will discuss messages our grandkids, adult kids, and spouses need.)

One type of toxic relationship is co-dependency, where one individual continues to give and the other continues to take. This type of relationship is unhealthy and unhelpful. The enabler is not helping a person change their circumstance but instead works to get the taker to rely on them even more. If this relationship is not adjusted, it can become enmeshed. An enmeshed relationship is overly connected. The individual is so entangled in the relationship that they lose touch with their own needs and feelings. Healthy boundaries are blurred, and family members have difficulty expressing their own thoughts or preferences when they don't line up with the family narrative.

A second type is low connection. It may occur when a grandparent has chosen to get involved only when necessary. This will result in the adult child feeling a sense of resentment. Even if the grandparent changes their tune, the adult child may not be receptive. This dynamic often occurs due to selfishness, but it could be unintentionally spurred on by distraction, inattention, or a chaotic schedule.[20]

"My daughter and her family lived in the same town as her in-laws. She had both her babies there. The in-laws would rarely visit their little grands. They maybe saw them once or twice a month. There was little effort made to check in on the family, see how they were doing, offer to babysit, etc. My daughter had each child via C-section. I came out before each child was born and stayed for three weeks after each birth. She really could have used some help after I left, and those grandparents did nothing. They didn't even ask my daughter how she was doing!"—Vanessa S.

"I'm estranged from my father. He abandoned us when I was about thirteen and my parents divorced. I tried to reconnect a couple times when I was in college, but he didn't have any desire to, so I let it go. Sometimes nothing can be done, and it is just better to move on. It wasn't my choice at first, but if he reached out to me, I would not want a relationship. No hate, no resentment, I have forgiven him but don't need him in my life."—Katie O.

Zero Connection

A third type of toxic relationship is zero connection. This is where we find the Checked Out and Canceled Grandparents. The Checked-Out personality chooses not to be involved as opposed to the Canceled grandparent who is prevented or blocked from being involved. In both cases, if the grandparent wants to reenter the family fold, that grandparent must seek relationship with the adult child and their spouse first. For a relationship to be rebuilt, apologies and forgiveness need to be part of the package. Own your part if you want a relationship, even if you think your behavior is not so bad or not such a big deal. Let go of pride or righteous indignation and begin to construct a relationship bridge.

When zero connection results from grandparents being canceled, it is most likely there is a wound that needs healing and trust that needs to be restored. Reconciliation, in my opinion, is better than a boundary of zero connection. That said, if physical or sexual abuse is the reason, the boundary will likely need to remain in place. Even if extensive therapy has been done, never leave the child alone with this person.

"I grew up with a father who had anger issues and a mother with a lot of passive aggressive tendencies. This made for a big dysfunctional family life. My parents separated when I was in college. At one point, my father said he had changed, but then he had a run in with my sister. I wrote a letter to him after that, saying I forgave him, but I couldn't be around him. I told him, I wanted him to get therapy and until he did, I didn't want any contact with him. He sent back a letter saying he was sorry for 'whatever he did.' My mother has her own issues. She developed a lot of behaviors because of the marriage, but it has recently come to light that she also has a lot of her own unresolved issues from earlier in life. If we try to set a boundary with her, we get shut down, or the silent treatment. My own kids have asked why grandma is so angry all the time. We still see her, but the relationship has become more and more distant."—Linda H.

Conditional Connection

This is the quid pro quo in relationships, getting something for something. "What do I get for it?" "What have you done to earn my love?" "You don't deserve a hug." "Because you were so awful we are not going to___."

This type of interaction may show itself in the personalities of the Captain or Chum.

"One of my kids was having a meltdown in the car. She was a toddler at the time. Her grandmother, my mother-law, said to her, 'If you don't stop crying, we are going to leave you here on the side of the road.'"—Lisa A.

Conditional connections expect conformity through control or threats. Our grandkids need to know we will never leave nor forsake them, no matter their behavior or attitude. They need to feel secure in the fact that our love, our relationship, is not conditional. Grandparents who lean toward the Captain or

Chum personalities need to be careful to avoid the traps of a conditional connection relationship.

Surface Connection

Surface connection is most often displayed in the grandparent personalities of Ceremonial or Cool.

"My mother-in-law is a hard person to get along with. We have had falling outs more times than I can remember. I keep my distance. I will text her. She has a wonderful son. I keep her informed for moments like her grandson's graduation. I wish her Happy Mother's Day and text on holidays. I send pictures and gifts. But she is not my favorite person. I have a name for her, but I won't share that here."—Laurel E.

Manners and proper protocol, in some families, may trump connection. Yes, manners are important, but stretched to the extreme have the potential to stifle relationships. Placing the focus on respect and honor are deeper character traits to build upon as opposed to the surface display of proper manners. Consider the child's age and stage. Our reaction to bad manners needs to be measured accordingly. If the parents are around, the manners instruction is best left to them. As grandparents we can model good manners and demonstrate how to respect and honor others.

Independent

"I want to raise my kids to be independent." This is a statement uttered with confidence. I often hear this from young parents in my coaching practice. I hear parents of adult children lament, "Well I raised my kids to be independent. I guess this is what that looks like."

You may be among many Americans who have raised children to be independent. Independence, after all, runs through our western veins. It's possible you fall into the grandparent personality of Captain; a person who highly values good behavior. What parents have come to understand is they really did not want the independent outcome. Complete independence results in separation from them. I want a relationship that lasts a lifetime. I want to be in my adult kids' lives and I want to be in my grandkids' lives. So rather than focus on the quality of independence, reinforce the characteristic of responsibility. Yes, responsibility is the quality I hope to reinforce in my grands.[21]

Jody M. describes her experience, "Before I had kids, I didn't see my parents or any family for almost three years due to my dad telling me to go be homeless when I was in a rough situation. I was between jobs and apartments. I have never been close to anyone in my family. However, we did talk about three years ago and have had casual conversations, nothing deep. Once I became pregnant, we moved to be closer to family in hopes that we would get support. Honestly my parents are willing to help when asked but they do not seem interested in getting to know me or my husband as people. They refuse to have difficult conversations. I am not trying to keep my children away from my parents. It is a two-way street, if they don't ask to come see their grandkids then I won't make the effort to take them. I invite them to come to stuff, but they always say no. It makes it hard to want them involved. I want them to make an effort."

Interdependent Connection

This connection can be seen in all the grandparent personalities except for the Canceled or Checked out. Interdependence is God's healthy model for family relationships.

"Some people even get angry when I tell them my daughter, her husband, and their preschool son live with us. Many people have said cruel things. Some are even Christians. They will say things like, 'Jason needs to support his family.'"—Rosemary V.

Aren't families meant to support and help each other? God created us to be interdependent, to be each other's helper. Shouldn't we be able to be our adult children's helpers if they run into hard times? I know several people who feel embarrassment or even shame admitting they have their adult children and grandkids living with them. Families need to stand together. Why wouldn't we help our adult kids if they need assistance?

For those grandparents who have adult children plus grands in their home, this is a chaotic and blessed time; it's an opportunity to have a big impact on their grandkids' lives. This may be a gift from God.

Currently, our eldest daughter is living with us. She ran into some hard times and needed a helping hand. We were happy to offer it. Interdependence is a "one for all and all for one" type of attitude. I believe this is a biblical family relationship.

Grand Merge

I'm sure you noticed; we are not the only grandparents in our grands' lives. There is another set from the other side of the family. The merging of different families and differences in the way they connect has the potential to create some unexpected issues. How families celebrate holidays, give gifts, express their faith, and interact will most likely be different. Those differences can create tension and must be respectfully and openly discussed. Our adult children may choose a way different from how they were raised. They can do this; we can accept this and learn another way.

In our home we chose to avoid recognizing Santa and the Easter Bunny, but we still had stocking gifts and Easter baskets. We chose a different way to celebrate those holidays from how we were raised. I think both sets of grandparents thought it was odd, but they respected our decision. Once we were asked, "If you don't do Santa and the Bunny, why do you do the tooth fairy?" Fair question. "The tooth fairy does not distract from Christ's birth or His resurrection. The tooth fairy is all about make believe." Open dialogue is important. Respect, and maybe not agreement, for how the parents choose to raise their kids is critical.

Grandma Wars

Families do things differently and so do grandparents. Some grandparents would like their way to be seen as the favorite or best way.

Many grandparents confess they feel threatened, insecure, or jealous when it comes to their grandchildren and the other set of grandparents' relationship with them. Rivalry for the grandkids' time and affection begins to fester. One set of grandparents notices the other has more access to or more privileges with the grandkids. Another notices that the other grandparents spend more on gifts. Some find it very tempting to make negative or disparaging comments about the other set of grandparents. Don't.

"My daughter's family lives five minutes from her in-laws and three hours from my husband and me. Our grandson sees his other grandparents almost daily. We see him as often as we can. From time to time a part of me gets to feeling sorry for myself. We are thankful for Facetime!"—Rebecca T.

Try to readjust your thought pattern to, "How nice my grand has so many people to love him." Speak well of the other set of grandparents. Do not put your adult children in a position to intercede or to carry the burden of grandparent competition. Each grandparent needs to find their relationship sweet spot with their grandkids and connect that way.

"It's the Grandma Wars," Kelly M. described the dynamic between her paternal and maternal grandmothers. "My grandmothers are in competition to be the favorite." Even though the two women were fast friends, each felt a little jealousy regarding the other's relationship with the grandkids. Things that typically stir jealousy among grandparents are noticeable differences in time spent with the grands, gifting, special grandchild knowledge, the number of pictures on display, and overt affection. Parents can help alleviate some of the comparison by spreading the love; even out those photos and access to the grands a little more evenly. It will never be exactly equal but work to close the gap as much as possible.

It helps to recall we have our own unique relationship with each grand. Find the connection that is uniquely yours, capitalize on that and weave the Christian Coach into that relationship.

"My daughter is close to her in-laws. Closer than she is to us. That hurts. Now my daughter has a baby, and I am wondering what that will look like going forward. I didn't picture this stage of life to be like this."—Brenda V.

Unmet expectations have the power to cause us deep pain. Speak your expectations, without involving the other grandparent. This is a more constructive way to go. Rather than, "You spend more time with ____." Switch it up to, "I'd love to have more time with ____." Keep the other set of grandparents out of the conversation.

"We are not the first ones they call. I sort of get it. It's natural for my stepdaughter to call her mom first. But when she does call us to watch the girls, our answer is always, 'Yes.' Even if we must change our plans or adjust our schedule. We take what we can get."—Valerie H.

Perspective in many cases can lead to peace. Perspective, love, and humility are qualities that have the power to improve relationships with the other set of grandparents. The better your relationship with the other grandparents, the more supportive each grandparent is of the other.

"My daughter's mother-in-law, the other grandmother, has brain cancer. Her prognosis is not good. I've told Alyssa, my daughter, during these upcoming years to always put Debby, her mother-in-law, first when it comes to holidays, not knowing how much longer Debby will be around. I want Debby to have first dibs on everything while she's still able to enjoy the children and grandchildren."—Lisa W.

The Favorite

I do not like the idea of singling out a favorite grandkid. Each one is special, each connection is unique. The Lord warns us about favoritism. In Genesis with Joseph and his brothers or with Jacob and Esau, we can clearly see how choosing favorites creates jealousy, which brings out the worst in people. Jealousy moves us to sin.

I recall a time when my daughter was in fourth grade and her teacher told her, "You are my favorite." My daughter believed her and felt proud of the fact she had a special relationship with this teacher, until she realized she didn't. She overheard her teacher say, "You are my favorite," to another student. This is not the way to win anyone's heart. Love them all, love them big. Some families like to joke about who is the favorite. I dislike this type of banter. For some reason my adult kids like to joke around like that. Perhaps they get a kick out of it because I don't.

I have observed each one of my adult children think someone other than themselves is the favorite. After one of my girls announced she was pregnant with baby number three, one of my kids jokingly said, "Now she has moved into first place." (Oh brother.)

It is tough to keep things exactly equal, but it is important to be aware of places imbalance may occur. Here are some things that grandparents can do to eliminate the idea of favoritism: spend the same amount of money on gifts for all the grands, as much as possible try to spend an equal amount of time with each child, display pictures of each grandchild, focus on the grandkids you are with rather than talk about the others unless asked.

"My parents have passed. My husband's mom is not that close to my son. She has chosen one of her ten grandkids that she likes." —Ellen C.

The merging of two different families is complicated and has the potential to stir comparison and jealousy. The level of relational satisfaction is impacted by the idea of fairness or balance in time or gifting. Imbalance and favoritism breeds jealousy.

If we want to have satisfying, healthy, and interdependent relationships with our adult children and grands, cultivating God's spiritual fruit in ourselves is a great place to begin. The apostle Paul defines healthy spiritual people and relationships in Galatians 5:22–23. The fruit of the Spirit is love, joy, peace, patience (forbearance), kindness, goodness, faithfulness, gentleness, and self-control. I need to ask myself, "Is my fruit sweet or spoiled?" It is up to me, with God's help, to bring sweet fruit to the family table.

Imbalance and favoritism breeds jealousy.

Love is patient, love is kind. It does not envy, it does not boast, it is not proud. It does not dishonor others, it is not self-seeking, it is not easily angered, it keeps no record of wrongs. Love does not delight in evil but rejoices with the truth. It always protects, always trusts, always hopes, always perseveres.

1 Corinthians 13:4–7

Grand Reflection

1. As you review the different types of family dynamics, in what areas are you doing well? Where could you improve?
2. Have you experienced feelings of jealousy regarding the other grandparents? What can you do to strengthen your relationship with your grandkids and avoid having favorites?
3. In Galatians 5:22–23, Paul lists the nine ingredients of good fruit. How would you characterize your fruit? Where could you improve?

Grand Verses

Read, reflect, and respond to these verses:

- Genesis 25:27–28
- Genesis 37:3–4
- Proverbs 27:4

What do you learn from these passages?

Grand Partner Tips

- Give your love generously to all your grands.
- Apologize, ask for forgiveness, and repent for past mistakes.
- Be sure to be as equal as you can be when it comes to showing interest in your grandkids and gifting them.

Grand Prayer

Heavenly Father,

> Thank you for Your example of how to love well. Grant me the courage and humility to address past mistakes. Give me Your wisdom and strength to repair relationships that are broken. Amen.

Chapter 3

Grand Shift

"WHEN THE CHILD YOU LOVE HAS A CHILD YOU LOVE WITH ALL THAT IS WITHIN YOU, ONLY THEN WILL YOU KNOW JUST HOW GRAND BEING A GRANDPARENT TRULY IS."

Have you pondered the definition of a nuclear family? It is a family unit made up of father, mother, and their children who live under one roof. The extended family goes beyond the nuclear family. This includes grandparents and aunts and uncles. A family of origin is defined as the family unit in which one is raised. Jesus even made this distinction between family of origin and the nuclear family in Matthew 19:4–6, "Haven't you read," he replied, "that at the beginning the Creator 'made them male and female,' and said, 'For this reason a man will leave his father and mother and be united to his wife, and the two will become one flesh'? So they are no longer two, but one flesh. Therefore what God has joined together, let no one separate."

Fellow Boomers and Gen Xers, we are no longer in charge. We are now in the family of origin and extended family categories. We are not members of our adult kids or our grandkids nuclear family. Our adult children have formed their own nuclear family with their spouse and children.

How do we encourage healthy interdependence while our adult children work to successfully merge two different families of origin? Respect, kindness, and flexibility are three characteristics that are called for as we make the grand shift from nuclear to extended.

I loved being the mom and having my kids all under one roof. I also appreciated calling the shots for my family. Tom's voice and mine were the ones that mattered when it came to decisions about finances, food, functions, and fun. As Mimi, I remind myself, "Lori, you are not the parent. You are the grandparent. These kiddos are my children's children." My grip must release because someone else holds the reigns. It is time for me to embrace the grand shift and slide to the side.

Embrace the grand shift and slide to the side.

Control or Influence

The statement, "The struggle is real," is almost cliché. Yet it captures what is true for many of us. The shift is a struggle, and it is hard. As a parent, we are used to having more control, which is appropriate for that time in our lives and our children's. As we enter the grandparent arena, grandparenting expert, Larry Fowler, warns against the attempt to maintain or utilize control.

Tom and I attended Larry's Grandparenting Matters seminar at Grace Church in Arvada, Colorado. Larry used an illustration of a scale.[22] On one end was control and the other influence. If the scales tipped toward control, influence was less. Conversely if the sales tipped toward influence, control was less. The implication is clear. The more we attempt to assert ourselves the less influence we have. "You must interact differently with your adult child than you did when they were in your home."[23] In his book *Overcoming Grandparenting Barriers*, Larry challenges grandparents to let go of control and identify personal controlling responses such as reparenting, blaming, guilting, and justifying. He encourages his readers to gain influence through strengthening relationships; the better the relationship we have with our adult children the more they are receptive to our influence.[24]

Mimis and Papas, Gigis and Poppies over the years we have gained life experience. Because of this our perspective is different from our adult children's. Time has also given us the gift of forgetting how emotionally charged some experiences can be. Compassion and wisdom are called for.

We adopted our first child from Colombia (we had three more the old-fashioned way) in the spring of 1988. She was very sick with a stomach virus. Due to this we needed to hydrate her throughout the night, drip by drip, using an eye dropper filled with homemade Pedialyte. We were in a foreign country and new parents. Tom and I were afraid our daughter would either need to be hospitalized or worse, die. Even though she survived the experience without hospitalization, Tom and I were shaken. In the fall of the same year, we took a road trip from Minnesota to Wisconsin. We planned on celebrating Thanksgiving with some of Tom's extended family and his mom. Our daughter, Courtney, came down with a fever. We, well for sure me, went into panic mode. It didn't matter that we were among two moms who collectively raised nine kids with one of the women being a pediatric nurse.

"She'll be fine. It's just a little fever. If you need to go to the hospital, it is just down the street." Logic and wisdom held no solace.

"She almost died when she had a fever before. We need to get home and see her doctor." There was no reasoning with a frightened new mama.

Of course, their statement was true but there was no dissuading me. They didn't agree but understood our resolve to go home. This scene could have been problematic if they had continued to persuade us to stay. Instead, they stopped problem-solving and demonstrated compassion.

Their compassion stands out. Our adult kids do not have the life experience we do. And we (I) need to give compassion for whatever the circumstance happens to be. I have not always done this well. I recall one time taking my little grand out in the stroller and getting home after his mom returned from work.

"Where were you? I was so worried. I almost went out looking for you." She was new mama frantic.

"We were just out, of course we were coming back." I did not demonstrate compassion and understanding at that moment. I wish I had.

Unsolicited Advice

Wisdom comes with life experience. Wisdom gained is specifically for the person receiving it. It may not always be for dispensing. I saw a meme that said, "Unsolicited advice is like someone singing out of tune. Nobody wants to hear it." Another quote that I think really captures what unsolicited advice sounds like to the recipient is, "Unsolicited advice is viewed as criticism."[25] If your kids do not ask for parenting tips, avoid sharing them. There are even times when advice is sought but it backfires, as was the case for Bonnie B.

Bonnie explains, "My daughter asked me to weigh in on the home she and her husband were considering. The location of the home was next door to her husband's parents. I cautioned her about the location and the potential loss of privacy. I'm not certain but I believe she communicated my concern to her in-laws. I was mortified. My shared wisdom may have done some relationship damage. I wish I had not weighed in."

Bonnie followed up by saying, "I've learned, even if I am asked my opinion, it does not mean it will be held in confidence. Whatever comes out of my mouth has the potential to be shared with another. I will keep this hard learned lesson in mind the next time my opinion is sought."

Lessons From Moses and Jethro

Giving advice does not always go south. Moses and Jethro are great examples of being a humble recipient and a compassionate dispenser of wisdom.

Moses was exhausted. He was leading the Hebrews as they attempted to navigate life. He was God's chosen leader and an adviser, judge, and jury for the people of God. Jethro was Moses' father-in-law. In Exodus 18, it is clear the two men had a mutual respect and love for each other. When they first came together after a period of separation, Moses briefed Jethro on all the miraculous things the Lord had done in the Hebrew's rescue from the Egyptians and Pharoah. Jethro listened, rejoiced, praised, and sacrificed to God for all the great things the Lord did. Later that day, Jethro had a meal with Aaron, the elders, and Moses.

The following day, Jethro observed Moses serve as judge for all the people. The people stood in line from morning till evening to have Moses settle their disputes or help them seek God's will. Jethro felt concern for Moses. His observation caused him to investigate the situation further. He began by asking Moses a couple questions before offering advice, "What is this you are doing for the people? Why do you alone sit as judge, while all these people stand around you from morning till evening?" (Exodus 18:14).

Moses replied, "Because the people come to me to seek God's will. Whenever they have a dispute, it is brought to me, and I decide between the parties and inform them of God's decrees and instructions" (Exodus 18:15–16).

> Moses' father-in-law replied, 'What you are doing is not good. You and these people who come to you will only wear yourselves out. The work is too heavy for you; you cannot handle it alone. Listen now to me and I will give

> you some advice, and may God be with you. You must be the people's representative before God and bring their disputes to him. Teach them his decrees and instructions, and show them the way they are to live and how they are to behave. But select capable men from all the people—men who fear God, trustworthy men who hate dishonest gain—and appoint them as officials over thousands, hundreds, fifties and tens. Have them serve as judges for the people at all times, but have them bring every difficult case to you; the simple cases they can decide themselves. That will make your load lighter, because they will share it with you. If you do this and God so commands, you will be able to stand the strain, and all these people will go home satisfied.' Moses listened to his father-in-law and did everything he said (Exodus 18:17–24).

As I read this account, I am struck by the relationship between the two men. Prior to providing advice, they spent time together sharing their lives. Moses seemed eager to tell Jethro all that the Lord had done, and Jethro was equally as intent to listen. Jethro spent time with the people closest to Moses and shared a meal with them. The following day, Jethro observed Moses burning the candle at both ends. His concern caused him to ask a couple of questions, then supply an alternative to the current situation. Jethro was not critical; he stated what he observed and had a solution to the issue. He started with connection then moved to correction. He matter-of-factly, without a critical spirit, shared his concern and a possible solution then he went on his way. Jethro did not hang around to micromanage his son-in-law's application of his recommendation. Moses was a humble recipient, and Jethro was a compassionate mentor.

This story is a great example for us personally and as in-laws. When we are the recipient (rather than the giver) of someone's hard-earned wisdom, it is good to consider it.

"Is this a word of correction from the Lord? Does it line up with my beliefs? Am I humble enough to consider there could be another way of managing a particular situation?"

When we are the recipient, be like Moses and have the ability and humility to hear another's recommendation. Ask God to give you the ability to discern wise godly advice from harmful advice. As the advice dispenser, be like Jethro. Connect first and be sure the suggestions come from a place of humility, love, and concern. Ask, "Are you open to hearing a suggestion?"

Once we become a Glama and a Boppa, the control officially shifts to our adult children. We move into a supportive role, following our adult children's lead. We ask before offering insight and give advice when asked. Scripture encourages us to let empathy and wisdom lead the way, "Therefore, as God's chosen people, holy and dearly loved, clothe yourselves with compassion, kindness, humility, gentleness and patience" (Colossians 3:12).

At this stage of life, many of us feel more like Jethro, inclined to give rather than receive advice. Yet, like Moses we should be ready to humbly accept correction and direction, no matter our age.

I did a very informal survey of my Moms Together Facebook group, a group where moms and grandmoms gather, and asked the moms, "What are your hot spots regarding your children's grandparents?" Here is the list of their top twelve frustrations. You will notice respect and control permeate their concerns:

- ***Don't respect their parenting style***

Many parents today parent differently from how they were parented. Just as we parented differently from our own parents. This is not necessarily a critique of how we did things, rather an informed choice derived from their own family's needs, past experience, resources read, and the culture. G-Mas and G-Pas, let's follow our children's lead and avoid being offended. They have put a lot of thought into how they want to discipline or correct their kids, just as we did.

"I wish my children's grandparents respected my parenting decisions." —Mandy D.

"My parents chose to spank, withhold dinner, and put my kids in the corner for not eating. They said, 'Our house. Our rules.' We stopped going to their house. Instead we had them come to ours."—Jill C.

- ***Do not support screen time limits***

Parents today work hard to monitor their children's screen time experience. Mental and emotional safety, device addiction, negative cultural messages, and immoral influences are some reasons parents limit technology. According to Pew Research, two-thirds of parents say parenting is harder today than twenty years ago. Many of those who responded cited technology like social media and smart phones as the reason.[26]

- ***Drop by unannounced***

Living near our grands is a grand privilege. If we happen to be blessed enough to live close by, we must be careful not to take advantage of the geographical closeness. Our grandkids and their parents have busy schedules, days filled with school, extracurricular events, lessons, naptime, mealtime, church activities, and family and friend time.

- ***Are unavailable***

"I wish my children's grandparents were more involved and would be more of a support for us."—Sandy S.

"I wish my children's grandparents made any kind of effort at all to get to know them."—Jessica K.

"My husband's parents have seen our kids so few times we can count the visits on one hand. I have seen them post online that they miss the kids and wish they could see them. They live less than ten miles away!"—Julie G.

Grandparents, it is up to us to respectfully and politely instigate connection and to carve out time to be available and accessible.

- ***Ignore gift giving specifications***

Most grandparents love to gift their grandkids. Some parents have boundaries regarding the type of gifts their kids receive. Be respectful of the parents' wishes to build trust.

- ***Disregard dietary restrictions and sleep schedules***

Disregarding food practices and sleep schedules can create tension and conflict. Because grandparents do not bear the main responsibility of the grandkids' diet and sleep, sometimes liberties are taken. This requires lots of communication between the parent and grandparent. "What are the restrictions? Are there times this can be flexible?" Talk it over, do not take over. Notice the choices the parents are making and have items of the same kind in your pantry.

"My mother-in-law offered to babysit, then gave my exclusively breastfed daughter formula for the weekend because she thought breast milk was disgusting. My daughter ended up severely constipated and colicky for a full week."—Jackie B.

"My parents sort of abided by our rules but they did not really like them. They gave our kids way more sugar than we appreciated, allowed TV beyond our rules, and did not discipline the way we asked them to. It would take about two weeks to detox them from a trip to their grandparents. Now I'm a grandmother and I see how hard it is to navigate all this. My daughter asks me to do this or that. I try to honor her wishes."—Anna M.

- ***Share photos on social media after asked not to***

Our grands are growing up in a world where there is little privacy. Many kids under the age of nine already have a digital footprint. Baby photos, videos of a toddler tantrum, first days of school documented, and more are available online. This concerns many parents. They are doing their best to protect their children's privacy and safety by managing what is shared on social media. Get permission before you share those cute photos.

- ***Withhold information about their time with their grandchild***

I think one of the worst lines spoken between a grandparent and grandchild is, "What happens at Grandma's stays at Grandma's." Teaching kids to not disclose information to Mom and Dad encourages the lie of omission. This puts parents in the enemy category while the grandparents and grandchildren are the allies.

- ***Contradict or undermine parent***

If Mom or Dad say, "No," no it is. If you have a reasonable request and would like Mom or Dad to reconsider, discuss your idea privately with them. Avoid contradicting the parent in front of the child.

- ***Disclose private information about the parent when the parent was growing up***

Some grandparents get a kick out of telling negative stories (which they now think are funny) about their child to their grandchild. This typically occurs when the grandchild is in middle school or older. Always paint the parent in a positive light. If the parent wants to tell their child about the time they threw an unsupervised party, that's up to them.

- ***Show favoritism***

This is a big hurtful problem. Each family is unique, and each relationship is precious. Attention, affection, affirmation, and gift giving should be as equal as possible.

"I wish my children's grandparents had a good loving relationship with my kids."—Leslie H.

- ***Laugh when the child is being corrected***

Okay, I confess, this can be a tough one to live out when our grands are littles. We feel like most everything they do is adorable. When they have that little stinker face or say something that is a little out of line, we want to chuckle. This is not helpful to the parents who are attempting to teach their kiddos respect and socially appropriate behavior. You may need to excuse yourself, so your grand does not see your reaction.

- ***Don't ask for permission to clean or do laundry***

I saw a comment on Facebook where a woman was mortified when her mother-in-law, while folding laundry and came across her "delicates." The mother-in-law commented on the undergarments, "Oh! There's not much left to the imagination, is there?" Yikes. Ask for permission before touching the laundry.

- ***Lacks sensitivity to parental or grandkid challenges or struggles***

We forget how hard parenting day in, and day out can be. In my Moms Together group on Facebook, the seasoned Moms and Grandmoms are reminded to be sensitive to the physical exhaustion parents of littles experience and the emotional toll raising teens can take. Have empathy and keep the perspective talk to yourself unless asked.

- ***Do not give unsolicited advice***

Even giving advice when it is sought can be tricky. Weigh your words carefully if you are asked to chime in.

"I feel I don't do things like they want. I really try. They don't take into account my health issues. They will confront me, 'in love' of course, with things they don't like or agree with. So mostly I don't say too much, instead I just pray through it."—Alison L.

When we embrace the grand shift from parenting to grandparenting, it is a blessing for our adult children, our grands, and for us. Our partnership with our adult children is not 50/50. We function in a limited partnership role rather than a general partnership. We are not equal, yet our impact can be eternal if we use the wisdom God has given us.

"I bite my tongue daily. I thought if once every ten years I came to them with something that I would have more pull. Apparently, I do not. I am just going to have to be more prayerful."—Leslie W.

Set a guard over my mouth, Lord;
keep watch over the door of my lips.

Psalm 141:3

Grand Reflection

1. Where or when is it difficult for you to let go of control?

2. How can you strengthen your relationship with your adult children and grandchildren?
3. Are you open to correction from your adult children? How do you respond to their criticism?

Grand Verses

Read, reflect, and respond to these verses:

- Titus 2:2–6
- Exodus 18:1–27
- Ephesians 4:2
- Matthew 19:4–6

What do you learn from these passages?

Grand Partner Tips

- Grand Be's
    - Be interested.
    - Be responsive.
    - Be available.
    - Be positive.
    - Be discreet.
    - Be supportive.
    - Be encouraging.
    - Be respectful.
    - Be interactive.

- Be sensitive.
- Be fair.
- Be kind.
- Be loving.
- Don't be the boss.

Grand Prayer

Father,

> Help me to let go of the parenting reins and embrace the grandparenting shift. You blessed me with the opportunity to raise my children, please remind me that You are now calling me to be a support and an encourager to my adult children as they raise their children, my grandchildren. Amen.

Chapter 4

The Grand Gap

"GRANDPARENTS EXPERIENCE A DOUBLE DOSE OF EXCRUCIATING PAIN WHEN THEY ARE ESTRANGED FROM THEIR CHILDREN AND CUT OFF FROM THEIR GRANDCHILDREN."
—LORI WILDENBERG

I gave my daughter-in-love a big hug of thankfulness yesterday. I was working on this chapter regarding family division through broken relationships, opposing political views, mental illness, or differing religious or worldviews. Many women who emailed or messaged me shared their heart-wrenching stories.

Grandparents experience a double dose of excruciating pain when they are estranged from their children and cut off from their grandchildren. According to Gransnet research, one in seven grandparents are estranged from their grandchildren, with many more estranged from their adult children.[27] My heart aches for those of you in this place. Sadly, this is not uncommon where different beliefs and worldviews exist.

If you are in this heartbreaking situation, I pray you find healing. Ways to bridge the barriers you are experiencing are provided in this chapter. The enemy is all over this. Have hope, we know, ultimately God wins.

Grand Separation

The division of belief systems is a tough hurdle. In 2018 and 2019 according to Pew Research eighty-four percent of the Silent Generation (born 1928–1945), seventy-six percent of Baby Boomers (1946–1964), and sixty-seven percent of Generation X (1965–1980) identified themselves as Christian.[28] That figure dropped to forty-nine percent of Millennials (1981–1996) who called themselves Christians.[29] The Millennials are the parents of our grandchildren. Some of us have adult children in the Gen Z category. About one-third of Gen Z born in 1996–2012 are religiously unaffiliated.[30] This group is more likely to identify as atheist, agnostic, or nothing in particular. Many of the Gen Zers and all the Gen Alphas (2013–2025) are our grandkids. Thirty years of disaffiliation and faith deconstruction contributes to what is being called the Faith Generation Gap.

Daniel A. Cox's article, "Generation Z and the Future of Faith in America," found at the *Survey Center on American Life*, says one in five Boomers read religious stories or Scripture once a week as their kids were growing up. Millennials and Gen Zers, twenty-four percent and twenty-one percent respectively, are more likely to engage in this way. Forty-eight percent of Boomers prayed or said grace before meals with their families at least once a week versus forty-two percent Millennials and forty percent of Gen Zers.[31]

"We struggle to see some of our grandchildren who are estranged from us due to divorce. It is a delicate dance because one parent is an atheist. I have made journals for the grandkids we do not see. I also buy and keep birthday cards and presents, hoping one day we will give these to them when they are old enough to make their own choices."—Mary P.

Our grandkids are growing up in a post-Christian culture. What does it mean for a society to be post-Christian? According to *GotQuestions.org*, the eroding reliance on Christianity makes it easier to justify beliefs and behaviors the Bible condemns.[32] It is important for us to be aware that our grandkids are growing up in a culture steeped in relativism (no absolute truth) and hedonism (the pursuit of personal pleasure).

Grandparents, we have our work cut out for us. It feels overwhelming, and we may experience great discouragement and despair, but trust God and recall these four truths:

1. Our grandkids were born for such a time as this.

2. Their parents are uniquely gifted to raise the children the Lord has given them.

3. Our impact on our grand's faith is second to Mom and Dad.

4. God wins.

Think of the sadness Samson's parents must have felt as Samson went against God's will and violated his Nazirite vow. (Judges 13–16 tells the full story of Samson.) Samson married a forbidden Philistine woman who eventually betrayed him. He had a pattern of giving up his faith for lust or love. His parents discussed their concerns with him, yet Samson went his own way. His parents continued to love him, even when he walked away from the Lord. In the end, Samson finished well. Perhaps, all the good things Samson's parents poured into him at a young age plus God's grip on Samson brought him back to the Lord. This story provides encouragement to pray, love like Samson's parents, and trust the Lord.

Like Samson and his parents, Susan and Kent have a great relationship with their daughter. They have differing belief systems, but their mutually respectful relationship overcomes this barrier.

"My daughter tells me she does not believe in God. She and her husband are raising their kids to believe there is no God. I think she still has a little bit of a belief. During a health crisis she wanted prayer. Our daughter is respectful of who we are. We don't shove faith down the grandkids' throats, but we are intentional about prayer before meals, playing Christian music, and talking about God's beautiful creation with the kids."

It seems more typical for adult children to struggle with faith. However, in Jenny E.'s case, it is the grandparents' worldview that creates the division.

"I did not realize the differences of opinion between myself and my in-laws, particularly my father-in-law. He holds the belief that all churches and religions are cults. Once I had my first child, I started to think about our extended family's belief system. I noticed little things like the type of gifts given, atheist books on logic provided, or little comments like, 'We are here to corrupt your kids.' As my kids develop their Christian worldview, they are less eager to visit their grandparents. This difference has prevented connecting at a deeper level."

Even if our adult children have discarded the faith in which they were raised, God can still use us to influence our grandkids and even our adult children. We can still speak godly principles without quoting Scripture. For example, we can say, "Treat others the way you want to be treated" instead of "Do to others what you would have them do to you" (Matthew 7:12).

The demonstration of love and respect are bridge builders. Prayer is our best barrier breaker.

Grand Disconnect

It is surprising and hurtful when your kids walk away from a relationship with Jesus. The feelings intensify when relationships break down. Today's culture climate is contentious. Many millennials and younger generations are deconstructing their faith. Topics like politics, vaccines, and religion are toxic. Divorce, blended families, and death complicate already challenging relationships. In some cases, in-laws negatively impact family of origin relationships. Life is messy.

> **We can still speak godly principles without quoting Scripture.**

God cares about family relationships. He tells us to settle matters quickly and move to forgiveness and reconciliation. "Therefore, if you are offering your gift at the altar and there remember that your brother or sister has something against you, leave your gift there in front of the altar. First go and be reconciled to them; then come and offer your gift. Settle matters quickly with your adversary" (Matthew 5:23–25).

"We don't disagree much, but when we do, we deal with it right away." Lisa's family is operating the way God prescribes. Keep short accounts, handle disagreements respectfully, and resolve them quickly.

Unfortunately, not all families are able to resolve conflict in a constructive way. "When Covid came out, I did not get vaccinated. My son and his wife were very upset. I ended up in the hospital and almost died. But God brought me through. My son said this was my fault. My son is angry. I divorced his dad and remarried. This grieves me. I pray for them daily. I tried to ask for forgiveness, but he said that was not good enough, I have thought about sending my grandkids cards, but I don't know if they will get them."—Katrina L

Some families do not resolve conflict at all, instead they continue to move forward. "At one point my daughter-in-law cut off ties with us. It lasted about a year. We were still able to see our grandkids, but this made our relationship with our son and grandkids difficult. Suddenly she came back into our lives and acted as if nothing happened. God used that time of separation to grow me. When we functioned as a family again, I wanted to bring up the subject of the separation, but God told me to leave it alone and be thankful she was back in our lives. So, I kept my mouth shut. I have to be okay with not knowing."—Katie F.

"After my husband passed away, my daughters-in-law's grief turned to anger, anger against me. I have not spent Christmas with my kids or grandkids since my husband passed away four years ago. God wants me to forgive her and love her. When I lead with love, the enemy's attacks have less of a chance of working. Some of my grandkids are now young adults so I text them directly."—Shelley M.

Larry Fowler's approach in his book, *Overcoming Grandparenting Barriers*, encourages his readers to apply Jesus' grace and/or truth strategy.[33] With His disciples and with the Pharisees Jesus led with truth, but with sinners, He led with grace. If you have a loved one who has walked away from their faith, follow our Lord's example and begin with grace.

"My son and his wife are fantastic Christians and are amazing parents. They have a strong commitment to marriage and to raising their children in the Lord. The relationship between my daughter-in-law and me is strained. It breaks my heart. I cannot figure it out. I try, I pray, I try, and I pray. She wants to keep me on the outside."—Martha J.

"We have not been able to see our grandsons. At one point my ex-son-in-law would let us see his boys when they were with him or with his parents, until Covid hit. After Covid, my daughter told her ex-husband if he continued to allow us to see the boys or have any contact with them, she would not let his parents see the boys."—Celeste S.

"I have noticed my daughter-in-law has been very distant the last few months. There are no issues right now, but I am worried. I am afraid she will stop letting us see the kids, just because she does not want us to. She has some mental health issues, so we try to give extra grace. I think, she thinks, we are out to get her. Of course we are not."—Elizabeth D.

"I have not been able to be a part of my two granddaughters' lives. My son hung himself because his wife was cheating on him. She later moved and changed her phone number. It has been almost twelve years since I saw the girls! I trust God will provide the opportunity to connect with them. This has nearly destroyed me."—Brena M.

Grand Anger

Estrangement is shocking. Many parents of adult children will say, "I have not done anything. My adult child cannot even give me a reason why." In my research, I discovered estrangement does not only occur when there has been abuse. It can occur due to consistent toxic patterns, mental health issues, a singular episode, or differing worldviews.

Perhaps the parents did not abuse or abandon their child but instead gave daily doses of criticism or exerted extensive control. And now the adult child chooses to disengage with the hope of protecting their child.

The values of loyalty, responsibility, and obligation are now replaced by happiness and the perceived well-being of the individual.[34] The culture wars have moved into families. Some members determine that canceling or "being done with a person" is the way to resolve conflict. Many individuals are not able to manage the space where they can kindly and respectfully agree to disagree for the sake of the relationship. There are situations where grandchildren are used as pawns to coerce the grandparents to behave in a particular way.

Grandparents have limited power to influence reconciliation or impact healing. The adult child holds all the cards when it comes to underage grandkids. What the grandparent can do is to listen, empathize, and attempt to understand. In most cases, the formula for reconciliation has elements of taking responsibility, respecting boundaries, and seeking forgiveness. The deeper the wound, the longer it takes to heal. Find ways to build the connection bridge. Seek unity, look for the places where you can agree. Keep the interactions surface and engage in common interests.

If the adult child holds their ground and refuses to connect, prayer is your best response. I cannot imagine the pain this would cause a grandma's or grandpa's heart. But you will need to abide by the boundaries they have set in place to build trust. Keep a notebook or journal and write down prayers and thoughts for each grand. Do not let this stop you from living your life or engaging in your ministry. You may even "adopt" a grandkid, someone whose grandparents are geographically at a distance. The Lord can still use you to impact another child. This won't heal the hurt, but it will make a difference.

Women in the family impact relationships in a big way. Fellow grandmoms, daughters-in-law, and moms-in-law, we can be a bridge builder or relationship buster. An article in *Psychology Today* talks about women playing a central role in holding the different generations within the family together.[35] Women are the "Kin Keepers." They are more likely to organize family gatherings, text, call, send cards, gifts, and plan visits.[36]

We have a choice; will we be used by the Lord to build or destroy the family bridge?

Close the Gap

For many (maybe most) life today is not what was envisioned when our children were children. We expected our kids would grow up, live near us, love us, love Jesus, and love having us be a part of their lives. This is not always the case, even if we raised our kids in a Christian home.

The religious divide is a big challenge. Some grandparents are prevented from talking about faith to their grandkids. Respect, open communication, and prayer are the ingredients to maintain relationships with your adult children and your grandkids. These qualities build trust and increase your influence. Your influence will be less overt, more subtle. Lovingly hold fast to your convictions. You do not have to compromise your conscience or convictions while you respect another's opposing belief. Do what you can to partner with the Lord, it is His desire to draw your kids and grandkids to Himself, too.

The relational gap is the biggest hurdle of all. Do your best to resolve conflict in a quick and respectful way. Be humble enough to accept corrections from your kids, even if it hurts a little. If blocked from contact, the best thing you can do is pray. During the time of separation keep a notebook of your prayers and thoughts for your grandkids to hopefully give to them someday. The relationship with the grands hinges on the relationship with the adult kids. If your relationship with your grands' parents needs repair, do it. Cultivate your relationship with your adult children and their spouses.

How can we proactively wait during times of unresolved conflict? Brena offers her solution, "We put aside money for every birthday and Christmas that we miss. I know money cannot make up for us not being there, but I am hoping it lets our grandkids know that we wanted to be."

Lead with love, respect, and humility. Admit fault, demonstrate grace. Let go of the desire for equal fault sharing or blame. Listen rather than lecture. Discuss rather than debate. Have a dialogue not a monologue. Build the bridge.

Make every effort to keep the unity of the Spirit through the bond of peace.

Ephesians 4:3

Grand Reflection

1. How would you characterize your relationship with your adult children and their spouse?
2. Which barrier do you struggle with? How will you respond to this?
3. Are you a bridge builder or buster with your siblings, in-laws, or your parents?

Grand Verses

Read, reflect, and respond to these verses:

- Judges 13–16
- Philippians 3:12–14
- Romans 12:2
- Ephesians 4:14–16

What do you learn from these passages?

Grand Partner Tips

- Be respectful and humble in your interactions with your adult children.
- Be respectful of your adult child's beliefs and hold true to your convictions.
- Keep short accounts. Resolve conflict quickly.

Grand Prayer

Lord God,

You know all about painful separations. You experienced betrayal and abandonment. Give me eyes to see how You want me to navigate this difficult road. Provide opportunities for me to connect with my adult children and grandchildren. Help me to be a bridge builder not a relationship buster. I know Your desire is to draw my loved ones to Yourself. Awaken in them a desire to know You. Amen.

Chapter 5

Grand Reflection

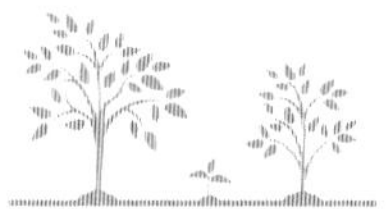

"I WANT TO BE THE PERSON MY GRANDKIDS THINK I AM."
—LORI WILDENBERG

We had one day left to enjoy our Minnesota lake vacation, then it was back to the Colorado mountains. Storms can rise up fairly quickly in the Midwest. A darkened sky and a big wind are the signals to get off the lake. As the weather was changing, Tom decided we had time to get the fishing boat off the lake and secured in the garage before the storm erupted. It made sense since we were leaving the next day.

I was grumpy, "The weather is changing, let's wait."

"No. Let's do it now, so we don't have to bail the boat later. We will not be using it again anyway."

Reluctantly, I got into the boat to go to the public access and meet my husband. Jaime, my daughter-in-love, accompanied me. Since the boat was out of gas, we needed to row. Jaime attempted to row but the wind worked against her. Rowing and wind are an incompatible duo. I jumped into the water to be the human rudder.

We affectionately call the bay where the public access is located, The Turtle Pond. It is full of turtles, both mud and snappers, a beaver resides there in a mansion not a lodge, and the water is weedy. Smart people avoid swimming in this part of the lake. But rudders must remain in the water. I could see Tom and our six-year-old grandson waiting for us on shore with the boat trailer.

My annoyance at my situation and at my husband grew. I was swimming in the swamp with weeds, the beaver, and the snapping turtles. Why couldn't we have waited to pull the boat out?

"This is so nasty. I'm not feeling very happy right now," I called out over the wind. My reflection looked a lot more like me and a lot less like Jesus.

"Mimi, why are you not happy?" My grand tuned into my words and tone. My husband wisely chose not to engage.

"Modeling. Roles models." Jaime quickly and good-naturedly articulated what was important in the moment.

Her words reminded me my grandson was watching this scene play out. I needed to demonstrate my ability to manage frustration and irritation with respect and self-control. Thankfully, Jaime spoke up and helped me put the swampy scene in perspective. (I think Tom was even more thankful.)

A Grand Image

As I look back on the swampy scene, God reminds me my spiritual fruit has some worms. My reaction to frustrating moments, disagreements, or suffering is often fleshly, not in the Spirit. I want to be the person my grandkids think I am. The person God has created me to be. I want to look more like my Savior and less like me.

God created us in His image. Together let's look at God's attributes to determine which areas in our lives need to be cultivated. God is relational, emotional, rational, volitional, and spiritual. We are made in His image and as humans we imperfectly bear those traits.

The omni qualities of God (omnipotent, omniscient, omnipresent) combined with Him being a thinking, feeling, and decision-making being makes Him one to honor and one who is worthy of our praise. Being created in His image we naturally desire to be respected. Some say that respect needs to be earned. I understand the reasoning behind this idea however, we are all worthy of respect because all are created in God's image. We must make the decision to interact with each other respectfully, even when we disagree or even when we are not treated with the same respect we are showing. Our grands must see us demonstrate godly respect to their parents, God, and to others.

Grand Feeling, Grand Thinking, Grand Acting

Like us, our grands are created in the image of a Holy God. They have strong emotions, thoughts, and preferences. And like us, they need to be transformed to reflect Jesus and live out those qualities in a godly way. We are all sinners in need of a Savior. The idea of living your "authentic life" is a worldly mantra. God is in the redemption and transformation business. Even when our behavior or our grands' actions are fleshly, it is up to us as grandparents to have a Spirit led response. We can choose to model how to feel, think, and act like Jesus.

What does it look like for a grandparent to look like Jesus?

- Keep promises.
- Use manners.
- Exhibit self-control.
- Listen.
- Speak truth.
- Show grace.
- Be gentle.
- Exude joy.
- Demonstrate kindness and goodness.
- Respond with patience.
- Use wholesome language.
- Provide opportunities for the grands to make some decisions.
- Behave in a way that honors God.
- Grant forgiveness; ask for forgiveness.
- Regulate emotions. Express anger, frustration, and irritation in a God honoring way.
- Share stories that show their parents in a positive light.
- Avoid sharing stories that embarrass or shame the grandchild.

We have a choice in how to respond in every circumstance. The ability to be spirit led results from daily surrender to the Lord. We may be saved, yet surrender is a moment-by-moment endeavor. Our grands observe how we interact with family members in complicated and weedy situations. I must submit my will and comfort to look more like Jesus and less like me. I pray my grands see Jesus in me. I want to be the person my grandkids think I am.

We have a choice in how to respond in every circumstance.

> "For I do not do the good I want to do, but the evil I do not want to do—this I keep on doing. Now if I do what I do not want to do, it is no longer I who do it, but it is sin living in me that does it. So I find this law at work: Although I want to do good, evil is right there with me" (Romans 7:19–21).

Grand Belonging

When we react in a fleshly disrespectful way to one another, relationships suffer. Respect and relationships are important to God; God is relational. The Lord did not create us because He needed us. He is self-sufficient and relational within the Trinity. The relationship among the Father, the Son, and the Holy Spirit, is a mystery to us. Even within the mystery, it is clear we are created for relationship by a relational God. We need to belong; we are created to need each other and need God.

My book, *The Messy Life of Parenting*, examines how independence rather than interdependence has seeped into family life.[37] "Independence frays family ties. An interdependent spirit knits our families closer."[38]

God created us to be interdependent, to need each other and to depend on Him. Belonging provides security. Our grands need to know they are a critical component of the family and of God's family. There are some kids who may never have a friend group, some may never be a part of a team, or a musical ensemble. Nevertheless, they need to know, no matter what, they are a critical and integral part of the family. As Grammies and Grampies how can we communicate this? Perhaps the best way is in small subtle demonstrations.

Here are some practical ways my grands know they belong and have a place at the family table figuratively and literally. Each grand has a personalized placemat, special silverware, plastic place settings, and a favorite-colored cup.

Their pictures are displayed all around the house: on the mantle, on the fridge, in the den, and in our bedroom. One of my grands placed a picture he framed of the two of us, right on my nightstand next to my bed.

Here are additional ideas:

- Create a photo book of grandkid-grandparent memories.
- Make those parent-approved treats!
- Put their artwork on your refrigerator.
- Wear the things they made or bought for you. (Tom and I each sport some pretty cool duck socks along with a beaded bracelet.)

- Have the grands participate in holiday meal preparation, table setting, prayer, conversation, and clean up.
- Play games as a family.

The Lord invites us to His table, He desires to adopt us into His family. Widen the family net and talk about God's invitation to His table and into His family. If they know Jesus, believe in Him, receive Him, and love Him, they are God's child too.

> "See what great love the Father has lavished on us, that we should be called children of God!" (1 John 3:1)

Grand Spirit

When we belong to a family, we share certain characteristics. Our Heavenly Father is spirit. As it says in John 4:24, "God is spirit, and his worshipers must worship in the Spirit and in truth." So often we nourish the body, feed the mind, and tend to emotions but forget to nurture the spiritual part of our being.

Spiritual nourishment comes in various forms. I spoke to my friend Mary about this. "Mar, how do you nurture your grands' spirit and help grow their faith?" I knew she would have an insightful and practical way to do this. She shared one of her family's favorite birthday activities.

"During a birthday dinner, each person tells of a special memory from the year with the birthday person, then they go on to talk about a personal, godly trait that the celebrated member has grown in and back it up with an example."

What a great gift for the receiver of these birthday messages. This tradition is so ingrained in their family that Mary's seven-year-old granddaughter asked at Thanksgiving, "Aren't we going to do our birthday celebration?"

The family, confused said, "This is Thanksgiving."

To which the seven-year-old replied, "It is Addie's birthday today. We need to celebrate Addie." (Addie is the family's golden retriever.) This birthday practice is now part of their family fabric.

Here are more ideas to strengthen our grand's spiritual formation:

- Learn a Scripture verse together.
- Let your grand teach you a verse he or she has learned.
- Share God encounters.
- Ask how each person made God smile today.
- Sing Jesus Loves Me.
- Sing worship songs together and include the motions.
- Read a passage from the Bible together.
- Pray before meals.
- Pray before bedtime.
- Go on a nature walk and discuss God the Creator.

My three-year-old grand and I learned a Scripture verse together. I used a technique called echoic reading. I would read or say a few words, and he would repeat those words. "In peace I will lie down and sleep. For You alone, LORD, [make me safe]" (adapted from Psalm 4:8). I treasure this special God-ordained moment.

Whether our grands live close or far, we can regularly show Jesus and exhibit His unconditional love, grace, truth, mercy, and justice. Even though we are an imperfect reflection of our Heavenly Father, God chooses to use us to point our grands to Him. When we daily (or even moment by moment) surrender our will, we look more like Jesus.

As water reflects the face,
so one's life reflects the heart.
Proverbs 27:19

Grand Reflection

1. How do you let your grand know he or she is a critical part of the family?
2. Which part of your Holy Spirit fruit needs some cultivation?
3. How are you nurturing your grand's spiritual side?

Grand Verses

Read, reflect, and respond to these verses:

- Genesis 1:27
- Galatians 5:22–23
- Psalm 139:4–12
- Psalm 147:5
- Isaiah 40:26

- John 21:17
- 1 John 3:20

What do you learn from these passages?

Grand Partner Tips

- Surrender to God's will and way each day.
- Show respect to your adult children in their role as parents.
- Learn a Bible verse with your grand.

Grand Prayer

Heavenly Father,

> Help me honor You by submitting my will to You each day. Transform me to be the person You have created me to be. Use me to draw my grands to You. Amen.

Chapter 6

Grand Messages

"GRANDPARENTS MAKE THE WORLD A LITTLE SOFTER, A LITTLE KINDER, AND A LITTLE WARMER."

We know firsts, we do not usually know lasts. I knew this would be my last time with Becky. She spoke. I wrote. Her words were filled with love, grace, and hope. Together we created five precious notes in all: one to her husband, one to each daughter, and one for both of her grandchildren.

"When do you want me to deliver these letters?"

"After..."

I was on holy ground. Sacred thoughts were expressed. I was honored to be in this thin space between Heaven and earth with my dear friend. Death clarifies things, doesn't it? The important becomes the immediate. The unimportant tossed aside.

Each note was unique to the recipient. Encouragement and love flowed within the words. A challenge and charge to embrace faith was given to each person. These written words were a gift, a treasure. Last words are powerful.

In Joshua 23, we read Joshua's last words to the leaders in Israel. He reminds them what God has done for them, what God has promised, how they are to act, and warns them to hold fast to God. The consequences of not obeying the Lord. Joshua declares,

> "Now I am about to go the way of all the earth. You know with all your heart and soul that not one of all the good promises the Lord your God gave you has failed. Every promise has been fulfilled; not one has failed. But just as all the good things the Lord your God has promised you have come to you, so he will bring on you all the evil things he has threatened, until the Lord your God has destroyed you from this good land he has given you. If you violate the covenant of the Lord your God, which he commanded you, and go and serve other gods and bow down to them, the Lord's anger will burn against you, and you will quickly perish from the good land he has given you" (Joshua 23:14–16).

Like Joshua, Becky communicated her thoughts and hopes to her family and friends throughout her life. Like Joshua, she was able to reiterate them with her last words. Those precious written words were expressed the day before she died. She wanted her family to remember good things and to focus on the important.

Grand Love

Love is where we start. Love is the place a faith journey begins. The recognition that we are loved not for who we are and what we do but for whose we are.

Love is the first of five critical messages your grands, adult children, in-laws, and spouse need—even crave—to hear. We must be careful to be like our Heavenly Father and love unconditionally. Our Heavenly Father's love for us remains constant no matter how we feel about Him.

We never want our loved ones to think they must earn our love, attention, or affection. There are two common errors to watch out for that could be interpreted by our grands as conditional love—comparison and favoritism.

"My son told me his grandmother said, 'I think your mom loves that dog more than you.' He then followed up by asking me, 'That's not true, is it Mom?' I confronted her and she denied saying that. I believe my son."—Amanda W.

Never compare your grands to each other (or to the pets). Each person is unique and comes with their personal gifting and unique struggles. Fully focus on each person when you are with that person, engage, get into their world, laugh together, and put down the phone. Time and attention speak love to our grandkids.

Steer clear of connecting behavior to security. We need to remember that God will never leave or forsake us, even when we are at our nastiest. Phrases like, "If you are not ready, I'm leaving without you" shakes a child to the core. Threats are a terrible way to get cooperation. Instead ask a question, "Do you need help?" or offer a motivation, "The sooner you get in the car, the faster we will get to the park."

Fear and threats are not the way to gain cooperation. Prior to a struggle, talk about being a team and discuss the idea of cooperation. This type of prevention reduces some of these frustrating episodes.

With each one of my grands I say, "Your mommy and daddy love you so much. Mimi and Papa love you so much. Jesus loves you so much." Then I break into song, "Jesus Loves You." Often when our time together comes to a close, I will say, "I love you, love you, love you." And of all the very sweet things, sometimes, my grands repeat this phrase back to me. We always have a choice in what we say. We can speak words that bring life or death. We can choose to say things that strengthen relationships or hinder them.

Grand Creation

Another message our grands need to hear is that God created them on purpose. Their life is not random.

While riding in the car, I was talking with my three-year-old California grandson,

"God created the ocean, the animals, the palm trees, and the flowers. He created these things for you to enjoy. God is the Creator."

My grandson nodded and repeated, "God is the Creator."

"Yes! God created your Mommy and Daddy, your two sisters, and YOU!"

"And Mimi and Papa?"

"Yes! God created each of us and He loves us BIG."

The conversation was short. I intentionally repeated the word, "Creator." I wanted my grand to catch the truth that God is Creator, and we are all created on purpose.

We arrived at our destination, Birch Aquarium in La Jolla. As we were looking in one large tank a dad and his preschool son approached the exhibit.

"That is the craziest fish I've ever seen. Is it dead?" The man seemed to know his way around the aquarium, so I thought he'd know the answer. The fish was flat as a pancake and its eyes were weirdly on one side of its body. It lay still on the bottom of the tank.

"No. It's a halibut. That's what they do. Lay in the sand."

"Whoa. I had no idea they looked like that."

"Yah, isn't evolution so interesting?" Not waiting for a response, he turned and walked away with his preschool-aged son.

Our grands need to know, they are not the random result of evolution, but they are created on purpose by a Creator who loves them.

Before we ate dinner that night, my grandson prayed, "Thank You for creating everything. Amen." Short conversations can be impactful.

"For you created my inmost being; you knit me together in my mother's womb" (Psalm 139:13).

Grand Purpose

God has created us on purpose, for a purpose. Our ultimate purpose is to glorify Him. This is an important message but a pretty tough concept for little ones. We can help our grands understand this concept a bit better when we deliver the idea that God gifts each person with unique character traits, and natural skills and abilities.

My friend Virginia speaks to her grandsons about how God has gifted each of them and how God can be glorified in their gifting. She began doing this when her first grandchild was two years old. He received a lot of affirmations, which is good. Yet Virginia thought perhaps those positive messages could go even deeper.

"You are so smart. You are so good at sports. Do you know why you are so smart and so athletic?"

"Why?"

"Because God is the One who created you and He is the one to give you those gifts."

Now that her grandson is eight years old, she asks a different question, "Do you know why God gave you those gifts?'

"No, why?"

"Someday God will show you how to use those talents to serve Him."

With another grandson who struggles with fear, she has a specific message for him,

"God gifted you in a way to learn to trust Him. God is not a God of fear. His gift to you is teaching you to trust Him."

And with a third grandchild, Virginia addresses the quality of being shy. Virginia herself was called shy as a child and says, "This labeling can create issues with self-worth, or it could be used as an excuse to be impolite."

"Shy is a word I never want to use with my grandkids. When I hear someone say, 'He's just being shy,' I respond, 'He's just taking time to take it all in.' Then later I say to my little grand, 'God gave you a voice. It is good to be polite and say, hi.'"

Later in our conversation Virginia told me how she used to respond when people would comment on her daughter's looks.

"Your girls are so beautiful,"

"Well, you should see their heart!" Virginia wanted her girls to understand that heart beauty is more important to God than physical beauty.

Virginia has given much thought to the messages she wants her grandkids to internalize. We too can be intentional like Virginia and speak words that encourage our grandkids and give them a better understanding of who God is and who He created them to be. The Bible reminds us, "we are God's handiwork, created in Christ Jesus to do good works, which God prepared in advance for us to do" (Ephesians 2:10).

Grand Capability

We love our grands with our whole heart. We know they are wonderfully and fearfully created to do good works. To do those good works, they need a God confidence in order to fulfill what God has planned for them.

Partner with the parents to build up a godly confidence in the children. Here are some ways in which that can be done:

- Offer encouragement.
- Provide sincere and specific praise.
- Make note of successes.
- Notice when they have persevered.
- Recognize the effort exerted.

Another somewhat controversial encouragement is the phrase, "I'm proud of you."

There are some parenting philosophies that steer adults away from saying, "I'm proud of you." One reason being the focus shifts from accomplishment to pleasing the parent or grandparent. Those concerned with this statement may say self-worth is hindered and a need for constant validation is created. Others consider, "I'm proud of you" patronizing. Adult-to-adult, that makes sense but not adult to child. An alternative could be, "You must be so proud."

Other philosophies encourage the phrase. Dr. Lee Bare in her article for *Psychology Today*, "Why Should Your Son Hear You Say You Are Proud of Him?" asserts it is important for children to hear you are proud of them. She says those words reinforce the values and behaviors that are important to your family, while showing them how to develop a sense of pride in personal accomplishment.[39]

Perhaps, the best way to communicate pride in your grand's successes is a mixture of the two philosophies. Be genuine and state your pride while backing it up with specific examples. Follow up with, "I'll bet that success feels really good." That way you get the best of both approaches.

Scripture tells us God says to us, "Well done good and faithful servant" (Matthew 25:21). That is another way of acknowledging a job well done. It is like saying, "Hey I'm proud of you and you are ready for more responsibility."

Grand Company

God tells us from Genesis to Revelation that He is with us. This is a message God repeats throughout the Bible. He wants us to know and to remember He is with us. He does not just exist as an uninterested observer; He wants us to enter a relationship with Him. He is our Father, our Friend, our Lord, and our King. He is not the Big Guy upstairs; He [God] is with us, beside us, behind us, and in front of us. He is with us in the good, in the bad, in the failures and triumphs, in the suffering, and in the rejoicing. "I am with you," is a message of confidence and security, our grands need to understand and embrace.

My youngest daughter was in a near fatal snowboard accident. As the medical team pulled her out of the ambulance to rush her into surgery, I asked God, "What do I say to her, Lord?" These might be the last words I would say to her.

God is with us, beside us, behind us, and in front of us.

"Tell her I am with her."

"Kendra, God is with you." I spoke to my unconscious child as they whisked her away.

"What…? That's what I say? Shouldn't I have told her I love her?"

"No, she knows that. She needs to know I am with her."

A couple of days, post-surgery, I was curious. Did Kendra hear me even though she was unconscious?

"Kendra, did you hear what I said to you before you went into surgery?"

"Yes, Mom. You told me, 'God is with you.'"

Then, almost as if on cue, over the loudspeaker at St. Anthony's Hospital the morning Scripture verse was read, "So do not fear, for I am with you; do not be dismayed, for I am your God. I will strengthen you and help you; I will uphold you with my righteous right hand" (Isaiah 41:10). We cannot always be with our kids and grandkids. It is critical they know their good God is always with them.

Grand Communication

The messages of unconditional love, being purposely created, having a purposeful life, having capability, and the knowledge that God is with us helps our grands step forward into life with confidence. These five critical messages speak life and fend off many cultural lies our grands will hear. The enemy attempts to destroy what God has created and calls good. He attacks their identity and their mental and emotional health. Identity, God's Word, and creation are typical targets for the enemy. In

Matthew 4 while Jesus was in the wilderness and had fasted for forty days, the devil arrived and asked him two questions that began with, "If you are the Son of God." The enemy attacked Jesus' identity in two of three temptations. In Genesis 3, the serpent places doubt concerning God's Word and challenges God's goodness, "Did God really say?"

> "Now the serpent was more crafty than any of the wild animals the LORD God had made. He said to the woman, "Did God really say, 'You must not eat from any tree in the garden'?"
>
> The woman said to the serpent, "We may eat fruit from the trees in the garden, but God did say, 'You must not eat fruit from the tree that is in the middle of the garden, and you must not touch it, or you will die.'"
>
> "You will not certainly die," the serpent said to the woman. "For God knows that when you eat from it your eyes will be opened, and you will be like God, knowing good and evil" (Genesis 3:1–5).

These five messages will strengthen your grands, adult children, in-laws, and spouse. They are truths your loved ones need to help them overcome hardship and suffering. When our kids know they are created on purpose, designed in a unique way, and belong to God's family, their identity is cemented in the Lord.

Words of life, eternal life, were the last words that came from my friend's lips. Her example of love and intentional messaging motivates me to speak words that reflect God's love, grace, encouragement, and hope to my family, my husband, my children, my in-laws, and my grands.

We may not have the same opportunity Becky and Joshua had to express last words. However, we can speak constant and consistent messages of faith, hope, and love to our grands.

And now these three remain: faith, hope and love.
But the greatest of these is love.
1 Corinthians 13:13

Grand Reflection

1. Which of the 5 messages do you communicate well? Where can you improve?
2. Where has God shown you that He is with you? Is this a story you can share with your grandchild?
3. What words or message do you want to regularly pour into your grands?

Grand Verses

Read, reflect, and respond to these verses:

- Joshua 23
- John1:1–3
- Psalm 139:13–16
- Ephesians 1
- Ephesians 2:10

What do you learn from these passages?

Grand Partner Tips

- Consider what would be your last words. Commit to communicating them now.
- Offer your grand regular genuine specific praise for effort, improvement, or success.
- Tell your adult children what a blessing and privilege it is to watch them be a mom or dad.

Grand Prayer

Father,

Thank You that You do not let us wonder if You are with us. Your Word tells us You are with us. Jesus' name, Immanuel, even speaks Your presence. Use me to build a God confidence in my grandchildren. Create an urgency in my heart to speak words of faith, hope, and love. Amen.

Chapter 7

Grand Prayers

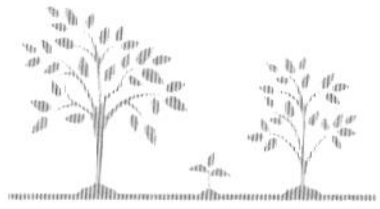

"INTERCESSORY PRAYER IS THE SWEETEST PRAYER GOD EVER HEARS."
—CHARLES SPURGEON[40]

"Mimi, we like doughnuts, don't we?" My three-year-old grandson looked up at me, with sugar clinging to his checks and fingers.

"We sure do. And Krispy Kremes are our thing!"

While my daughter, Samantha, and son-in-love Alex, were busy with new arrival number three, I took the two older kiddos, a three-year-old and a twenty-two-month-old on a doughnut date. I had never had one of those warm melt-in-your-mouth delights until then.

"Ma'am, would you like a membership?" A reasonable question given the fact that we had frequented the shop at least three times in about eight days. The three of us were becoming regulars. We even had our typical table, a corner table by the window. My grandson claimed his usual chair, my granddaughter popped into her spot, and I grabbed a chair from the table next to ours. This was becoming routine.

I declined the membership, only because that doughnut date was to be the last doughnut date we would have for a while. I was leaving the West Coast that day to head home to the foothills of the Rocky Mountains.

At every visit each child settled on a doughnut with pink frosting and sprinkles. I had what had become my usual, a standard glazed.

"Thank you for the doughnuts, God. Amen." This prayer from my grandson was as sweet as those Krispy Kremes. After we thanked Jesus for the deliciousness, we enthusiastically indulged in our morning treat.

Grand Thanks

Those doughnut dates brought feelings of joy and thankfulness to my heart and to the little grands' hearts. It did not take long for our doughnut date to become routine. Same order, same table, same chair, and same wonderfulness crossing our lips. It is a positive thing to have good, regular routines. Another good and regular routine is our prayers before a meal.

When our kids were young, they took turns being the one to pray before dinner. One of the sweetest memories Tom and I have of that prayer time is when our youngest prayed, "Thank you God for our family and our food. Then all the king's horses and all the king's men, couldn't put Humpty together again."

First Thessalonians 5:18 tells us to always give thanks to God for everything. God uses our prayers of thankfulness to tenderize our hearts, calm our minds, and draw up faithfulness in our spirit. When we pray prayers of thankfulness with or for our grands, we affect their (and our) heart, mind, and soul. Feelings of satisfaction and contentment come from a posture of thankfulness to God. We can model and teach our younger grandkids a short thankfulness prayer. Short prayers are easy to recall and repeat, "Thank you God for our family, our friends, our food, and Jesus. Amen." The older kids can take that prayer and expand it, adding in more detail. Make thankful prayers a habit to pray at mealtimes. Ask your grands to lead the prayer if they are comfortable. Never force it and refrain from grading the prayer. Rather than, "That was a good prayer." Say, "God smiles when you pray a prayer of thanks." Let's get away from evaluating prayers and instead encourage a conversational type of prayers.

Grand Peace

Encourage your grands to pray with you. Commit to pray for your grandkids. Fear of the dark and the fear of being alone are typical developmental struggles for little ones. We can remind our grands that God is always with us so we can be strong and courageous. Frame this verse and place it next to your grandchild's bed as an encouragement to trust the Lord. "Be strong and courageous. Do not be afraid; do not be discouraged, for the LORD your God will be with you wherever you go" (Joshua 1:9). When God provides insight into your grandchild's struggle, pray for them and find a verse to encourage them. Pray specifically for a spirit of courage and increased trust in the Lord.

Lord,

Help my grandchild be strong and courageous. Provide Your comfort and knowledge of Your presence and protection before my grand falls asleep. Amen.

Pray specifically for your grand's concerns, worries, or fears.

Grand Joy

Our prayers are not limited to talking to God about our grandkids' hardships or struggles. We can pray prayers of praise as well. One of my grands exudes great joy. So much I think it comes out of her pores. One day her hair was standing straight up. I believe all her joy was pouring right out of those blond hair follicles. The words of Nehemiah 8:10 capture her completely, "The joy of the LORD is your strength."

Father,

I praise You for the joy my grandchild feels and expresses. Thank You that joy in You is her strength. Amen.

Praise prayers are fun to pray aloud, "Jesus thank you for the beautiful sunrise. Amen." Make prayer a part of your time with your grandkids.

Grand Anger

If you have the privilege of being in your grandkids' presence, you will most likely have an opportunity to see them angry. As a kid, I had a reputation in my family for letting the fish caught at the family cabin go. I could not stand to see them in that big black container in the water, knowing the next thing they would experience was their demise. There were some natural fish escapees, others were dined on by a local racoon; to be fair some may have had some human born-free intervention.

My grandma was quite the fisherwoman. She would stand at the end of the dock with one or more of her grandsons and drop a line into the water. Next the fish would be taken off the hook and dropped into the large black cylinder holding tank next to the dock.

As the fish were corralled in the tank, I lay on the dock, looking through the dock slats at the free-swimming fish below me. My cross necklace dropped between the spaces as I looked at the water below. I jerked my head up, my necklace caught, broke, and fell into the water. I dropped down to look through the opening in the boards to find my necklace.

Gram thought (reasonably so) I was preparing to release fish. She called out, "Lori! Leave the fish alone. Stay away from the fish. Get off that dock."

I was upset about my broken necklace. I was not thinking about releasing fish. I was on a mission to find my broken necklace and now I was being told to get off the dock.

Tears spilled out of my eyes. I shouted back, "Just shut up, Gramma."

I marched into the cabin with my parents', aunt's, and uncle's disappointed eyes burning a hole into my head.

"I'm sorry I said shut up. My necklace broke and I was trying to find it in the water." Tears now streamed down my cheeks.

"I'm sorry too. I thought you were letting the fish go. I didn't know your special necklace broke." I never found my necklace that summer, but I did find my Gram's understanding, humility, grace, and forgiveness.

Our grandkids will get angry in front of us or maybe even at us. If we can view anger as a problem identifier rather than a solution we will be in good shape. We can teach our grands that anger can be a good thing. It indicates there is a problem. Our next step is to use that energy to find a solution to that problem, then implement grace and forgiveness as needed.

Lord God,

Help me and my grandkids not to sin in our anger. Stop us from using harsh words. Replace the harsh words with gentle words. Use me to help teach my grandchild how to handle disappointment and frustration. Amen.

"A gentle answer turns away wrath, but a harsh word stirs up anger" (Proverbs 15:1).

Grand Grief

God willing our grands will experience a full life. A life filled with fear, anger, joy, and sadness will be a part of their story. Of course, we want to delay the less pleasant experiences, but God will use those heartaches and struggles to mold our grandkids into the people He created them to be. Think of it, if our grands never had sadness, how would they develop compassion? If they never felt fear, how would they learn to be brave? If they were never angry, how would they learn to problem solve or to stand up for another person?

The thought of, "I only want my grandkids to be happy," is a low bar. A solely happy life would be a shallow, self-centered life. We can help our grandkids move through fear, express anger in a healthy way, and navigate grief well. Romans 5:3–5 reminds us, God will use their troubles to grow and shape them. "We also glory in our sufferings, because we know that suffering produces perseverance; perseverance, character; and character, hope. And hope does not put us to shame, because God's love has been poured out into our hearts through the Holy Spirit, who has been given to us."

The thought of, "I only want my grandkids to be happy," is a low bar.

We don't like to think of our grands experiencing grief. But they will. Death of grandparent, a parent, a sibling, a friend, or a pet. Death is something that touches us all. The finality of suicide, critical illness, and accidents creep into our lives. We want to shield our grands, protect them but what do we do when the harsh side of life moves into their sphere?

Grief is a tough emotion because it is often generated by a problem that cannot be fixed. Death is a grief producing experience that a grandchild cannot fix. I asked the women in my Moms Together Group on Facebook if they had any stories about how a grandparent could help a child in the grieving process.

One mom, Danae B., whose husband died, wisely said, "supporting the grandchildren also supports the mom." Danae went on to say, "My parents have been a huge source of support for me and my kids. My in-laws, not at all. It's been two years now and all they do is send birthday cards. At first, I was afraid they would take over. My mother-in-law would call me daily crying saying she needed to see the kids. Maybe she just wanted a physical reminder of her son. She was so pushy and intense I feared she would want to take the kids from me. Now she's basically absent. My parents are a safe space for my kids. If I tell my mom my daughter is having a bad day, she gets in her car, drives two hours to our home, and takes my eleven-year-old out for coffee or shopping. My daughter opens up, they laugh and talk, and act like best friends. My mom weaves faith into the conversation, reassuring my daughter that she will one day see her dad again. This gives my daughter peace. I believe kids need as much family as they can get during their lives. My daughter is definitely happier when she spends time with her grandparents."

Another mom, Kacey, who lost her mom (BB), grieves for herself and for her son. Her dad, who is also grieving, has been a healing presence in Rebel's life. When Rebel gets out of school, the first thing he says is, "I want to talk with PawPaw." They have a daily connection. Kacey says, "I know this has helped my son and it helps my dad too. They spend a lot of quality time together hanging out. Rebel's favorite thing to do is to spend the night at PawPaw's home on the weekends. It comforts Rebel to be in BB's home."

My friend Carla and her family experienced trauma and tragedy. A year after Carla's mom died, a mountain lion killed her friend's ten-year-old son. Their families were close. The loss was painful. Carla learned a lot during this time about how to help kids in the grieving process. She said, "The main thing to remember is that children process grief differently. My son wanted to talk about things and my daughter preferred to journal. We must be willing to communicate that nothing is off the table. We need to be ready to have uncomfortable conversations at inconvenient times. I think one of the critical messages to communicate is, no matter what you go through, God will be with you. We have a big God, and we want our kids to know that."

As I have listened to different stories about grief and loss, I realize a grandparent's presence is an important part of the healing process for grieving kids. Parents prefer the gentle support a grandparent can offer rather than an overwhelming reaction to the grandchild's pain. Follow the parents lead, be sensitive to the child's unique way of grieving. Ask both the parents and the grandchild what is helpful. Sometimes a distraction is the thing that is called for. Other times a conversation is needed. Listen to the need expressed. Don't take over. Sensitivity to the parent's and grandchild's needs, the opportunity for the grandchild to openly express feelings, and messages of encouragement stand out as important elements in the healing process. Psalm 116:15 states, "Precious in the sight of the Lord is the death of his faithful servants." God cares about our birth and our death. And we have His promise of eternal life through Jesus Christ. Sometimes God's promises or a heartfelt, tender Scripture is exactly what is needed, other times Scripture could be received as a platitude that discounts the child's pain. We can always speak God's truth and communicate His love even if we are not quoting the Bible.

Heavenly Father,

You are the God of all compassion. Thank You for being with my grandkids to comfort them when they grieve. Thank You that You are also with them when they are fearful, angry, and full of joy. Amen.

"I am with you and will watch over you wherever you go" (Genesis 28:15).

Grand Petition

Prayer regarding our grandkids' present feelings of anger, fear, joy, or grief are four ways to talk with God about our grandkids. There are additional things to pray about regarding our grandkids.

I created a list, for you and for me, of 15 topics plus Scriptures to pray for our grands. Insert your grandchild's name into the prayer.

1. Know Jesus

"The work of God is this: to believe in the one he has sent" (John 6:29).

Lord, I pray You work deeply in my grandchild's heart to know You. Amen.

2. Deepen Faith

"Therefore, rid yourselves of all malice and all deceit, hypocrisy, envy, and slander of every kind. Like newborn babies, crave pure spiritual milk, so that by it you may grow up in your salvation, now that you have tasted that the Lord is good" (1 Peter 2:1–3).

Lord God, draw my grandchildren to You. Give them a desire to have a close and deep relationship with You. Amen.

3. Relationship With Their Parents

"Honor your father and your mother, so that you may live long in the land the Lord your God is giving you" (Exodus 20:12).

Heavenly Father, I pray my grandchildren love, honor, and respect their mom and dad. Amen.

4. Choose Good Friends

"Walk with the wise and become wise, for a companion of fools suffers harm" (Proverbs 13:20).

Father, give my grandchildren the wisdom to choose good and godly friends. Amen.

5. Discover Their Purpose

"For we are God's handiwork, created in Christ Jesus to do good works, which God prepared in advance for us to do" (Ephesians 2:10).

Lord, provide my grandchildren an understanding of how You have uniquely gifted and specifically called each one to live out the calling You have on their lives. Amen.

6. Develop Godly Character

"But the fruit of the Spirit is love, joy, peace, forbearance [patience], kindness, goodness, faithfulness, gentleness and self-control" (Galatians 5:22–23).

Father God, grow the fruit of the Spirit in my grandchild. Amen.

7. To Have the Ability to Hear God's Voice

"My sheep listen to my voice; I know them, and they follow me" (John 10:27).

Lord, You are the Good Shepherd. I pray my grandchildren know You so well they recognize Your voice and follow You. Amen.

8. Discernment and Wisdom

"And this is my prayer: that your love may abound more and more in knowledge and depth of insight, so that you may be able to discern what is best and may be pure and blameless for the day of Christ" (Philippians 1:9–10).

Heavenly King, grant my grandchildren wisdom. Gift them with the ability to discern right from wrong and good from bad. Amen.

9. Courage to Do the Right Thing

"Be on your guard; stand firm in the faith; be courageous; be strong" (1 Corinthians 16:13).

Father, supply my grandchildren courage to honor You in all they think and do. Amen

10. Protection From Ungodly, Evil Influences

"But the Lord is faithful, and he will strengthen you and protect you from the evil one" (2 Thessalonians 3:3).

Faithful God, protect my grandchildren from the evil influences of this world. Give them the strength to stand against or flee from temptations. Amen.

11. Good Work Ethic

"Whatever you do, work at it with all your heart, as working for the Lord, not for human masters, since you know that you will receive an inheritance from the Lord as a reward. It is the Lord Christ you are serving" (Colossians 3:23–24).

Father, bestow the ability of my grandkids to persevere in hard things. To do chores or work as if they are working for You. Amen.

12. Contentment

"The greedy stir up conflict, but those who trust in the LORD will prosper" (Proverbs 28:25).

Giver of All Good Gifts, I pray my grandkids will trust You and be content in the ways in which You have blessed them. Amen.

13. Forgiveness

"Bear with each other and forgive one another if any of you has a grievance against someone. Forgive as the Lord forgave you" (Colossians 3:13).

Father, You are a God of forgiveness. I pray my grandchildren have the humility to ask for forgiveness and the love to give forgiveness. Amen

14. Love for God's Word

"Praise be to you, Lord; teach me your decrees. With my lips I recount all the laws that come from your mouth. I rejoice in following your statutes as one rejoices in great riches. I meditate on your precepts and consider your ways. I delight in your decrees; I will not neglect your word" (Psalm 119:12–16).

Lord God, grant my grandkids a love for Your Word and a desire to obey Your commands. Amen.

15. Honesty and Integrity

"For we are taking pains to do what is right, not only in the eyes of the Lord but also in the eyes of man" (2 Corinthians 8:21).

Lord, move my grandchildren to be honest in the small things so they can demonstrate integrity in the big things. Amen.

Spontaneous, rote, or routine prayers are all important. Praying with, for, and modeling prayer is all part of being a great and intentional Christian grandparent. Prayer is an act of love.

I have not stopped giving thanks for you, remembering you in my prayers.

Ephesians 1:16

Grand Reflection

1. With parental permission, when do you pray with your grandkids?
2. How do you typically pray for your grands?
3. Have you asked your adult children how you can pray for them? If not, ask.

Grand Verses

Read, reflect, and respond to these verses:

- 1 Thessalonians 5:17
- Proverbs 15:1
- Romans 5:3–5
- Joshua 1:9

What do you learn from these passages?

Grand Partner Tips

- Pray for your grandkids each day.
- With parental permission, pray with your grandkids each time you are with them.
- Pray for your adult children and their spouses.

- Pray these Scriptures for and with your grandkids. Ephesians 3:14–21; Philippians 1:9–11; Psalm 20:4; Colossians 1:9–14; Psalm 25:4–5.

  Father, I ask You to fill my grandchildren with the knowledge of Your will through all the wisdom and understanding that the Spirit gives, so they may live a life worthy of You and please You in every way: bearing fruit in every good work, growing in the knowledge of You, being strengthened with all power according to Your glorious might so they may have great endurance and patience, and give joyful thanks to You, their Heavenly Father, who qualifies them to share in the inheritance of Your holy people in the kingdom of light. For You, oh Lord, have rescued us from the dominion of darkness and brought us into the kingdom of Jesus Christ, in whom we have redemption, the forgiveness of sins. Amen.

  This prayer is crafted from Colossians 1:9–14

Grand Prayer

Father,

Thank You for the gift of my family. Give me eyes to see how I should pray for my adult children, their spouses, and my grandkids. Move me to pray to You daily for my family. Amen.

Chapter 8

Grand Blessings

"BLESSED IS THAT MAN WHO HAS DONE WITH CHANCE, WHO NEVER SPEAKS OF LUCK, BUT BELIEVES THAT FROM THE LEAST EVEN TO THE GREATEST, ALL THINGS ARE ORDAINED OF THE LORD."

—CHARLES SPURGEON[41]

"May the Lord bless you and keep you. May He make His face shine upon you and be gracious to you. May He lift up His countenance upon you and give you peace. In the name of the Father, Son, and Holy Spirit. Amen."

Tom and I prayed for our daughter, Kendra, and son-in-love, Collin, prior to them leaving for Argentina to climb Mount Aconcagua. After our prayer for God's protection and provision, we gave them the Aaronic or priestly blessing found in Numbers 6:24–26.

When my kids were young, I would say this blessing before they bolted out the door for school. I would complete the blessing by putting the sign of the cross on their forehead. Lately, I have been thinking it is time to impart this blessing on my grands as well.

Grand Blessings, Benedictions, Promises, and Responsibilities

In chapter seven we discussed how to pray for and with our grandkids. Here we delve into how to speak blessings over our grandchildren. This activity is done as grand partners with parental agreement and support. Blessings and prayers are slightly different. A prayer is communication with God that may involve adoration, confession, thanksgiving, and supplication. A blessing emphasizes God's protection and provision along with our happiness and peace.

As I researched biblical blessings, I discovered there are over 100 blessings and benedictions in Scripture. A benediction blessing is declared by a pastor at the conclusion of the worship service and is spoken over the entire congregation. It motivates, challenges, and commissions the congregants to apply the truth that has just been preached. Ephesians 3:20–21 is a good example of a benediction, "Now to him who is able to do immeasurably more than all we ask or imagine, according to his power that is at work within us, to him be glory in the church and in Christ Jesus throughout all generations, for ever and ever! Amen." This benediction verse can be used as a personal blessing with your grandkids during times when perseverance, bravery, or determination is called for. The benedictions we find in Scripture may be used as blessings.

A blessing is like a benediction, it can be given by any believer to an individual or group and is not limited to being spoken in a formal church setting. A blessing's goal is to guide the believer in righteousness and to offer hope. It usually begins with, "May the Lord."

To understand the difference between blessings and promises I compared the two. Promises in Scripture typically begin with God saying, "I will." Psalm 32:8 perfectly captures this idea, "I will instruct you and teach you in the way you should go; I will counsel you with my loving eye on you." Some promises can also be blessings. Promises are God's solemn word that what He says will be fulfilled. They are a one-way covenant, from God to us. We can't mess up God's promises by what we do, think, or say. God is a promise keeper.

A blessing may be accompanied by certain responsibilities on the receiver's behalf. Proverb 3:5–6 is a good example of personal responsibility and God's response to that, "Trust in the LORD with all your heart, and lean not on your own understanding; in all your ways submit to him, and he will make your paths straight." It is up to us to take that leap of faith and trust the Lord in our circumstances. Speak this blessing over your grandchildren and explain their part in seeing God's blessing unfold. God will show your grandkids the way when they trust Him with all their heart and obey His will and way.

Grand Blessedness

A beatitude is the condition of being blessed usually by a pastor or ministry leader in a group setting. Jesus revealed God-given spiritual rewards during his Sermon on the Mount found in Matthew 5:3–11. He counters the culture and addresses a believer's condition and God's response to it.

Worldly Value	Followers Traits	God's Blessing
Independent, pride	Poor in spirit (those who humbly realize their need for God)	Receive the kingdom of Heaven
Hedonistic, personal happiness	Mourn	Comforted
Power abuser	Meek or gentle	Inherit the earth
Personal rights	Desire righteousness	Satisfied
Strength minus compassion	Merciful	Receive mercy
Deceitful (anything to get ahead)	Pure in heart (devoted to God, sincere intentions)	See God
Personal satisfaction	Peacemaker	Called sons of God
Tolerant	Persecuted for righteousness (holds fast to convictions)	Inherit the kingdom of Heaven

God cares about how we live out His command to love others. The blessings given in Matthew are the result of how God responds to the way we live our lives and love others.

A beatitude is a tender blessing that can be spoken over your grandchild in times of suffering or struggles. Be sensitive to their emotional state when doing this. We don't want to discount their heartache or hardship. "Blessed are you for the mercy you have shown. You will receive mercy from God." Or "Blessed are you as you mourn, God will comfort you." The beatitudes remind us that no matter our circumstances we can still experience hope and joy.

Grand Spirit

Our struggles can result in God-given blessings. Like those found in Isaiah 11:2–3: wisdom, understanding, counsel, might, knowledge, and fear of the Lord. Or the Holy Spirit provides spiritual gifts, which are given at conversion. One place we can find a list of spiritual gifts is in 1 Corinthians 12:7–11: wisdom, knowledge, faith, healing, miracles, prophecy, discernment, tongues, and the interpretation of tongues.

"There are different kinds of gifts, but the same Spirit distributes them. There are different kinds of service, but the same Lord. There are different kinds of working, but in all of them and in everyone it is the same God at work" (1 Corinthians 12:4–6). First Corinthians 14:1 encourages believers to earnestly ask God for a spiritual gift, "Follow the way of love and eagerly desire gifts of the Spirit, especially prophecy." Solomon asked God for wisdom, and this pleased the Lord. He blessed Solomon with the spiritual gift of wisdom.

These spiritual gifts are given by God for the common good and to glorify Him. These blessings come with responsibility. It can be easy to forget that the blessings are not for us to hold onto tightly but rather to loosely embrace. These gifts are to be used to build up God's kingdom, draw others to the Lord, and glorify God.

Grand Gifts

When you are given a gift, how do you respond? Are you able to say, "Thank you" or do you feel uncomfortable because you felt undeserving of the present? Ephesians 1:1–19 tells of the many gifts the Lord bestows upon us, His people, who are in Christ. Scripture says we are blessed with every spiritual blessing, chosen before time, predestined, adopted, redeemed, forgiven, and marked with a seal. The Lord calls us His own. He fully knows us and fully loves us from eternity past to the present, and beyond. Our grandkids need to grasp this truth. They do not have to earn God's love; they are worthy because God says they are. Paul concluded the Ephesians passage this way, "I keep asking that the God of our Lord Jesus Christ, the glorious Father, may give you the Spirit of wisdom and revelation, so that you may know him better. I pray that the eyes of your heart may be enlightened in order that you may know the hope to which he has called you, the riches of his glorious inheritance in his holy people, and his incomparably great power for us who believe" (Ephesians 1:17–19).

"Glorious Father, bless my grandchildren with the spirit of wisdom and enlightened eyes so they may know You better. Amen."

Grand Living

We follow those we trust. If we want to impact our grands' lives, we must be worthy of their trust. Trust is earned. When someone betrays confidence, broadcasts failure, breaks a promise, or exhibits disloyalty, trust is broken. We earn our grandkids trust by keeping promises, not betraying a confidence (I am not suggesting we keep things from their mom and dad), not sharing their bad moments, and being loyal.

For our grandkids to understand that God is trustworthy they must experience that sort of trustworthiness in their lives from their parents and grandparents. Jeremiah 17:7 states, "But blessed is the one who trusts in the Lord, whose confidence is in him." When we are confident in the faithfulness of another, trust grows. When our grands learn we can be trusted they will transfer that to a trustworthy God and have confidence in Him, His Word, His way. We are blessed when we know God is a God who is faithful and trustworthy.

If we want to impact our grands' lives, we must be worthy of their trust.

Grandest Blessing

The biggest and best blessing of all is a blessing that is unearned and undeserved. Romans 5:8 states, "God demonstrates his own love for us in this: While we were still sinners, Christ died for us." This is the greatest good news, a message our grandkids must embrace if we are to come back together in Heaven. Academic achievement, athletic awards, musical talent, beauty, acceptance to an elite college, and a six-figure job, none of it matters if our grands have not received God's biggest and best blessing of all, faith in His Son Jesus Christ. This is the critical blessing to pray for, "Father, bless my grandkids to follow Jesus with all their heart, mind, and soul. Amen."

Grand Journey

Kendra and Collin successfully summited Mount Aconcagua. God was before them, beside them, and behind them. The Lord blessed them with excellent guides and protection from the big winds. Out of the forty trekkers only four summited. Kendra and Collin were two of the four. Prayers and blessings spoken over them were precious to them over the fifteen days of hiking up 22,831 feet.[42]

Words that come in the form of blessings are ways we can positively and supernaturally speak life and impact our grandkids. The words we consistently speak become a piece of the fabric of how they view God and who they see themselves to be.

Our grands may not climb any of the seven highest summits on each continent, but they will have their own journey with uphill battles.[43] Our part is to pour blessings over them and pray for them as they navigate their life.

To be an effective and authentic deliverer of God's blessings, we must know our Heavenly Father and His Word. We can choose to stay silent, speak discouragement and negativity, or we can speak life.

The tongue has the power of life and death.

Proverbs 18:21

Grand Reflection

1. Have you ever had a blessing spoken over you? If so, when, where, and by whom? What impact did it have?
2. What might prevent you from speaking a blessing over your grandkids?
3. When do you think the most practical time would be to bless your grandchild?

Grand Verses

Read, reflect, and respond to these verses:

- Numbers 6:24–26
- Psalm 20:1
- Psalm 90:17
- Psalm 115:15
- 2 Corinthians 13:14

- Colossians 1:9–11
- 1 Thessalonians 3:12–13
- 2 Thessalonians 3:5
- 2 Thessalonians 3:16
- Hebrews 13:20–21

What do you learn from these passages?

Grand Partner Tips

- Use the above verses to speak blessings over your grand. In some cases, the verbiage is slightly adjusted to make it more personal.
  - Numbers 6:24–26—May the LORD bless you and keep you; the LORD make his face shine on you and be gracious to you; the LORD turn his face toward you and give you peace.
  - Psalm 20:1—May the LORD answer you when you are in distress; may God protect you.
  - Psalm 90:17—May the favor of the Lord our God rest on you; may He establish the work of your hands.
  - Psalm 115:15—May you be blessed by the LORD, the Maker of heaven and earth.
  - 2 Corinthians 13:14—May the grace of the Lord Jesus Christ, and the love of God, and the fellowship of the Holy Spirit be with you.
  - Colossians 1:9–11—May God bless you with wisdom and knowledge of His will through the wisdom and

understanding the Holy Spirit gives. Live a life worthy of the Lord and please Him in every way: bear fruit in every good work, grow in the knowledge of God, be strengthened with all power according to His glorious might so you may have great endurance and patience.

- 1 Thessalonians 3:12—May the Lord make your love increase and overflow for each other and for everyone else, just as mine does for you.
- 1 Thessalonians 3:13—May He strengthen your heart so that you will be blameless and holy in the presence of our God and Father when our Lord Jesus comes with all His holy ones.
- 2 Thessalonians 3:5—May the Lord direct your hearts into God's love and Christ's perseverance.
- 2 Thessalonians 3:16—May the Lord of peace Himself give you peace at all times and in every way. The Lord be with you.
- Hebrews 13:20–21—May the God of peace, who through the blood of the eternal covenant brought back from the dead our Lord Jesus, that great Shepherd of the sheep, equip you with everything good for doing his will.

Grand Prayer

Lord, cause me to memorize these blessings from Your Word. Create in me a holy habit of speaking Your blessings over my grandkids each time I am with them. Amen.

Chapter 9

Grand Holiday Fun

"IF YOUR HEART OVERFLOWS WITH LOVE FOR GOD, YOU WILL FIND A THOUSAND WAYS TO COMMUNICATE AND PASS ON THESE FEELINGS TO YOUR CHILDREN."
—IRENAEUS

"How do you weave faith into your family holidays?" I posed this question to the moms and grandmoms in my Moms Together Facebook group. One mama, Sammie, wisely said this, "I think if you try to fully saturate your home with your faith, you'll find that the holidays are easy to blend in with your faith."

The more we bring faith into our family's daily life, the more natural it is to let faith-filled activities and conversations flow during the holidays. Even if we have not yet begun the daily walk and talk about faith with our grands, we must start somewhere. Holidays are a great place to kick off faith-based activities and conversations.

In Leviticus God lays out a clear schedule for the celebration of Holy Days, times when God's people gather to recall His faithfulness and goodness. The celebrations and feasts were instrumental in passing along faith to the next generation while deepening the individual's belief. Traditions are a powerful way to pass along our faith to our grandkids.

Holidays and celebrations are a big deal to us grandparents. Expectations of the entire family gathering on a special day are high, and perhaps unreasonable. Feelings get hurt, disappointment is experienced, and frustrations mount. Flexibility is called for. Before we move into practical ideas for being the Christian Coach at family gatherings, let's discuss some guidelines first.

1. Be flexible. Just because it has typically been done one-way does not mean we are unable to change. Remove your Captain or Ceremonial Cap and replace it with the Consultant one. It is up to us to listen to our adult children's needs and create a less stressful schedule. Our adult children feel pulled and tugged if both sets of the grandparents live locally. Be willing to step back and follow your adult children's lead. Celebrate a holiday on a different day or make life convenient and invite the in-laws to be a part of the get together. Our son and daughter-in-love like to reserve Christmas morning for their own little gang. We must be supportive of their efforts to create some of their own traditions. Respect their decisions, just as we wanted our parents to respect our holiday choices.

2. Be willing. We can be the travelers if our grands do not live locally. It is typically harder and more expensive for the parents and kids to come to the grandparents rather than us go to them.
3. Be creative. If you cannot travel, you can still Face Time and make use of the mail system. Last Easter, we were not able to be with our West Coast grands, so I mailed items for their Easter basket plus created a faith-based scavenger hunt for them to do with their mom and dad (see the Easter section for more details).

Be flexible, be willing to travel, be creative. Be grand partners.

Birthdays

One of our out-of-town grands happened to be with us near his birthday. Since we are not usually able to celebrate his birthday in person, we decided to throw him a three-year-old family birthday party. The birthday party theme was construction. Decorations, paper plates, napkins, party favors all related to the construction concept.

We added the underlying concept of identity. We pray our grands are confident in who God created them to be. The culture tells us who we are is who we choose to be, who other people say we are, or what we do. None of these three ways are biblical. God tells us who and whose we are.

Around the idea of God-given identity, I created a scavenger hunt for the cousins. Clues for the next find were in an envelope labeled with a specific child's name. That way each child had a turn to open a clue.

Each of the twelve identity treasures had a trinket or treat to go with it and a biblical truth attached to it. An envelope for the next clue was also with the treasure. They would load up their bag with their identity loot, listen to the next clue, and run to the next location.

I am God's child. John 1:12—fruit snacks

I am a friend of Jesus. John 15:15—teddy grahams

God chose me to be in His family. 1 Peter 2:9—goldfish crackers

God created me to do good works for Him. Ephesians 2:10—coloring book

I am made in God's image. Genesis 1:27—slime

God protects me. 1 Peter 1:5—sunglasses

God loves me, no matter what. Romans 8:38–39—stickers (I used monkey stickers)

I am God's special creation. Psalm 139:13–16—bubbles

I am precious to God. Isaiah 43:4—animal crackers

God sings over me. Zephaniah 3:17—apple juice

God is always with me. Hebrews 13:5—light up toy

God makes me strong and helps me. Isaiah 41:10—peanut butter crackers (if you have peanut allergies in your family use something else)

Nine of the declarations begin with "I am." Those statements reinforce the truth that God chooses our identity. The last three are truths about God for grands to embrace. Understanding who they are will clear away the confusion the enemy attempts to throw their way. Even if you don't host your grand's birthday party, you can plan an Identity Scavenger hunt for another time. If you print out the verses and laminate them, they could be taped to the bathroom mirror to reinforce the idea that our identity is in Christ. When our grands are rooted and established in God's truth, their ability to discern lies from truth increases.

New Year's Day

> "Therefore, if anyone is in Christ, the new creation has come: The old has gone, the new is here!" (2 Corinthians 5:17).

New Years is a great time to discuss the idea of transformation with your grands. Use the caterpillar to cocoon to butterfly as your example. God can transform us into a beautiful creature when we ask Him to renew our mind. On a piece of paper draw a caterpillar, cocoon, and a butterfly. Let your grand color the pictures and talk about the change that occurs in the cocoon. Relate that change to growing up and maturing in Christ. Ask, "What do you think God may be teaching you now?"

Another conversation would be to talk about past and present things to be grateful for and hopes for the future. I found this New Year's prayer over at No Greater Joy on Facebook, "God help me to be grateful for what You did in the past, mindful of what You are doing in the present, and hopeful about what You are going to do in the future." [44] Share this prayer with your grandchild.

Valentines

The story of St. Valentine is an inspirational account we can share with our grandkids. St. Valentine, a Roman priest, defied an edict around AD 269 from the emperor Claudius (a persecutor of the church) that prohibited marriage.[45] Valentine secretly married young couples. The emperor's reasoning for the law was, unmarried soldiers fought better than married soldiers. He assumed married soldiers would be more fearful of dying because they had families.[46]

Eventually, Valentine was imprisoned for performing marriage ceremonies and sentenced to beatings, stoning, and decapitation because of his stand for Christian marriage. Asterius was one of the men to judge him. The judge had a blind daughter who Valentine prayed to receive sight. According to legend, she was healed. Ultimately, Asterius became a Christian due to this miracle. The last words Valentine penned were in a letter to Asterius's daughter, which he signed "from your Valentine."

Valentine's story is about having courage to stand up for your beliefs and sacrificially love God and people. The love Valentine expressed was agape love—selfless and unconditional.

"We taught the historical account of St. Valentine and then made cookies for the residents in the nursing homes." Moms Together member Andrea focused on the reason we celebrate

Valentine's Day and included an act of service to demonstrate love. Tell the story, figure out an act of service and do the act.

Parenting expert, Dr. Emily Scott shares how her family celebrates valentines, "We either cut out hearts or buy a cheap box of Valentine's cards. Each day of the week, we write notes to one another saying kind words or why we love each other. Then we tape those notes to each person's bedroom door. One year we focused on Jesus' love and shared Bible verses about love." We can tweak Emily's idea and use this with our grands. Provide a box of valentines and have each grand write down their words of blessings to their siblings and to their parents. Encourage them to share these valentines throughout the week leading up to Valentine's Day.

As Omas and Opas, we can give our grands the love gifts of service, affirmation, presents, hugs, time together, and sacrifice, and encourage them to show love in the same way.

St. Patrick's Day

Just like with St. Valentine, tell the story of St. Patrick. When telling Patrick's story, we see that many biblical characters have similar accounts. At sixteen, Patrick (an English boy, not an Irish) was taken prisoner (like Daniel) by Irish pirates. Like Daniel (Daniel 1), Patrick did not abandon the faith he grew up with. He was a shepherd slave for six years (other biblical heroes who experienced captivity: Joseph, Daniel, Shadrach, Meshach, Abednego). God told him in a dream to escape and he returned to his home in England. (Others with dreams or visions: Joseph (Genesis 37–42), Joseph (Matthew 1–2), John (Revelation 1, 9),

Peter (Acts 10–12) Paul (Acts 16–18.) He received faith training for fifteen years, became an ordained priest, and returned to Ireland. He used a shamrock to teach the Trinity.[47]

Include a conversation about the armor of God from Ephesians 6:10–18 to reinforce the concept of bravery in a spiritual battle. With your older grands, a game of Fact or Fiction would be fun to play on St. Paddy's Day prior to telling his story. For example:

Fact or Fiction—St. Patrick was captured by pirates. True or False?

Fact of Fiction—St. Patrick was Irish. True or False?

This builds anticipation and interest.

Easter

"We do a sort of Advent for Easter beginning thirteen days before. I have a handmade Resurrection Egg Set along with Scripture to read each day leading up to Easter."—Sammie Walker

Grandparents, we may not be able to do the daily activity, but we can modify this idea. You don't have to make your resurrection eggs; you can purchase an already assembled carton that includes Scripture verses to go with each egg. Inside each egg is an easter symbol like a donkey, whip, or nail.

I created an Easter Egg Hunt for my grands, similar to the Identity Birthday activity. Each grand got an empty egg carton to fill. Each station had an egg for each child with the same item in each egg along with a Scripture verse to be read before consuming the treat or playing with the toy.

Egg #1—Fruit snack, Galatians 5:22–23

Egg #2—Raisins, Psalm 34:8

Egg #3—5 Pennies, Psalm 20:7

Egg #4—Rolo with the gold wrapper, 1 Peter 1:7

Egg #5—Goldfish, Matthew 4:19

Egg #6—Younger kids Baby Shark finger puppet, Genesis 1:26. Older kids Paw Patrol finger puppets, Deuteronomy 31:6

Egg #7—Peanut butter eggs, Isaiah 34:15

Egg #8—Smiley face stickers, Proverbs 15:13

Egg #9—Sticker saying Friend in Jesus (you may not be able to find this. Substitute something else to represent friend), John 15:13

Egg #10—Lion, Daniel 6

Egg #11—Rainbow or boat, Genesis 6–9

Egg #12—Empty (empty tomb), John 20:1–10

Create a faith-focused and faith-building Easter basket for your kids. Include all or some of these twenty-five items with the corresponding Scripture reference in the basket. Each one represents a biblical story, gives a truth, or provides a promise of God.

Use numbered gift tags with twine and attach the verse provided to each gift. As your kids unpack their baskets, save the gift tags. For the next twenty-five Sundays your family can read and discuss the Bible passages in numerical order. All the verses are about Jesus' life, teaching, death, or resurrection.

1. Trail Mix: Deuteronomy 6:6–7
2. Magnifying Glass: Luke 1:1–4
3. Flip Flops: Luke 3:15–16
4. Squirt Gun: Matthew 3:13–17
5. Bible: Luke 4:14–21
6. Legos: Luke 6:46–49
7. Kleenex: Luke 7:11–17
8. Eraser: Luke 7:36–50
9. Seeds: Luke 8:11–15
10. Flashlight: Luke 8:16–18
11. Sunglasses: Matthew 17:1–8
12. Family Activity Coupons: Luke 10:38–42
13. Hairbrush or comb: Luke 12:6–7
14. Coloring book with crayons: Luke 12:27
15. Band-Aid® adhesive bandages: Luke 17:11–19
16. Juice box: Luke 22:7–23
17. Scented lotion or cologne: Luke 23:55–24:12
18. Red, white, purple, black, orange, green, yellow, pink jellybeans: Respectively: Romans 5:9; Isaiah 1:18; John 19:19; Romans 3:23; 6:23; Ephesians 2:8–9; Matthew 28:5–6; Revelation 21:21; Romans 15:13
19. Gardening tools: John 20:1–18
20. Goldfish crackers: John 21:1–4
21. Chocolate lamb: John 21:15–17
22. 40 Pennies: Acts 1:1–6

23. Bubbles: Acts 1:7–11
24. Worship music CD: Acts 16:16–40
25. Journal with a pen: John 21:24–25[48]

Mas and Pas, we can encourage our grands to remember Easter every day when we create a basket that can be enjoyed on Easter and beyond.

At Easter another Moms Together member, Sandy, prays this short and powerful prayer, "Thank you, Jesus, for dying on the cross for our sins." She repeats this prayer year after year. "When I am not on this earth any longer, the generation yet to be born, will hear those prayers as well."

Thanksgiving

Laura, a friend of mine, makes felt coasters. She gave me several of her designs. My favorites are the sunflower and leaf coasters. I have at least twelve. They are yellow, orange, red, and light brown, vibrant fall colors. Rather than use them as coasters I have attached "thankful" Scriptures to them. My grands set the table. They put one leaf or flower at each person's place. Prior to eating, we go around the table and read each verse. When the kids get older, this can be adjusted to having the kids say the Scriptures in their own words. The verses attached to the coasters are Psalm 107:21; Ephesians 1:16; Psalm 7:17; Psalm 9:1; Colossians 3:17; Romans 7:25a; Philippians 4:6; 1 Corinthians 1:4; 1 Chronicles 16:34; Psalm 69: 30; 2 Corinthians 9:15; and Hebrews 12:28. This places our focus on whom we are to direct our thanks.

Christmas

Recreating the journey Mary and Joseph took from Nazareth to Bethlehem is one way to encourage our grands to better grasp the Christmas story. It is easier to do this on a day prior to Christmas Eve or Christmas Day. The Bible briefly describes the journey from Nazareth to Bethlehem. This trek was a dangerous, difficult, and lengthy one.[49] Mary and Joseph needed to travel a total of ninety miles, ascending and descending the hills. It is reasonable to assume they only traveled ten miles a day due to Mary being well along in her pregnancy. It was winter so the weather would have been cold and rainy combined with freezing temperatures at night. The heavily forested areas along the Jordan were also home to lions, bears, and wild boars. There were also outlaws who targeted the major trade routes.

If you have stairs in your home, you can more easily replicate the up and down hill part of the journey. At each location have something for the grands to collect. Narrate the journey as they travel.

- **The Journey to Bethlehem**

"Your journey begins in Nazareth, Mary and Joseph's hometown. You will need to get all the way to Bethlehem, which is ninety miles away. This will not be an easy trip. You will need a donkey."

Nazareth was on the main level of our home. Each "traveler" received a plastic donkey.

"We need to go down the mountain so a walking stick will help."

The kids walked down the stairs, with their hiking stick, to the Jordan River Valley.

"Congratulations! You made it down the mountain. Now you are going to walk on a path filled with rocks and dirt, then you will go through a forest. Watch out for wild animals like lions, bears, or wild pigs."

At the bottom of the stairs each one got a rock to represent the unpaved path Mary and Joesph traveled on, then they ventured into the dangerous and heavily forested Jordan River Valley. Small stuffed animals like lions, pigs, and bears were the items found there.

We chanted and marched, "Lions, Boars, and Bears, Oh MY!"

The desert experience was next.

"Now you are in the desert. It's winter so it is cold and rainy." At this location a water bottle was discovered.

"You made it through the forest and the desert. Now you must climb the mountain to get to Jerusalem."

They ascended the stairs to Jerusalem and enjoyed a muffin.

"You only have five miles left to go to get to Bethlehem. This is your last day of the journey!" They made it to Bethlehem and then to the stable where they found baby Jesus. We celebrated when we found baby Jesus. Each traveler received a certificate for traveling ninety miles to see baby Jesus.

My grandkids ages five, three, and two had fun pretending to be on the journey. This activity will need to be repeated as they get older to better grasp the grueling journey from Nazareth to Bethlehem.

Other less involved things we can do include make a birthday cake for Jesus, sing happy birthday to Jesus, go look at Christmas lights and talk about Jesus being the light of the world, and read the nativity account in Luke 2.

Grand Planning

In order to have a successful holiday activity, we need both creativity and planning. On the next page is a template to help you organize your next special day with your grand.

A Holiday Planning Template for Your Use

Faith, Family, Fun, Facts, and Food Planner

- Holiday or Theme ______________________________
- Main Concept (What I hope my grands will learn) ______
  ____
- Themed Food ______________________________
  ____
  ____
- Supporting Scripture ______________________________
  ____
  ____
- Supporting Story ______________________________
  ____
  ____
- Activity
  - Littles: Scavenger Hunt, Storytime, Songs, Act it out, Other
    ____
    ____
  - Bigs: Fact or Fiction Guessing Game, Discussion, Other
    ____
    ____
- Prayer ______________________________
  ____
  ____
- Blessing ______________________________
  ____

Grand Days

With intentionality, Sandy, focuses her extended family non-holiday mealtime prayers on thankfulness and hope, "Thank You God for all You have done in our family. I preemptively praise You for what You are yet to do that we cannot see."

Regular practice, repetition, and tradition build faith. That is why God commanded all of Israel to celebrate three yearly feasts: Passover, Pentecost, and the Feast of Tabernacles. He wants His people to remember these events, to recall His faithfulness, and pass those stories along to their children and their children's children.

Regular practice, repetition, and tradition build faith.

The Jews took it on themselves to establish th custom that they and their descendants and all who join them should without fail observe these two days every year, in the way prescribed and at th time appointed. These days should be remembered and observed in every generation by every family, and in every province and in every city. And these days of Purim should never fail to be celebrated by the Jews—nor should the memory of these days die out among their descendants.

Esther 9:27–28

Grand Reflection

1. Why do you think God commanded certain festivals and feasts to be celebrated?
2. Which holidays can you infuse with more faith-based conversations or activities?
3. Which ideas presented here will you commit to use?

Grand Verses

Read, reflect, and respond to these verses:

- Esther 9:27–28
- Isaiah 12:6
- Matthew 26:18
- 1 Corinthians 11:25–26

What do you learn from these passages?

Grand Partner Tips

- Be intentional about bringing faith into your holidays.
- Support the faith activities your adult children are doing with your grands.
- Be flexible.

Grand Prayer

Father, keep me mindful of the reasons for each holiday and talk about those reasons with my grandchildren. Amen.

Conclusion

The Grand Gift

"BUT IN YOUR HEARTS REVERE CHRIST AS LORD. ALWAYS BE PREPARED TO GIVE AN ANSWER TO EVERYONE WHO ASKS YOU TO GIVE THE REASON FOR THE HOPE THAT YOU HAVE. BUT DO THIS WITH GENTLENESS AND RESPECT."
1 PETER 3:15

"Mimi, how old is Jesus?" my three-year-old grandson's eyes widened expectantly. We were getting ready to celebrate Christmas, Jesus' birthday. Asking how old someone is on their birthday is pretty common.

"What a great question! Jesus is forever years old." I extended my right arm and stretched it in a semi-circle.

"Jesus is four?" His brow furrowed.

"For ever. Jesus is even older than Mimi and Papa. Jesus was with God when God created the world." A tough concept but my answer satisfied him.

You never know when those faith building conversations will pop up. Our eldest grand, told me, "Mimi, I like it when you read Pops' prayers." My dad, Pops, who had his Heaven day years before my six-year-old grandson was born, wrote prayers in poem form. One year, for my dad's birthday, I collected his precious writings and created a book of them. I made an additional book for my family. It is a tradition to read one of Pops' prayers before our Thanksgiving, Christmas Eve, Christmas Day, and Easter meals. I had not realized my young grandkids paid attention to this, let alone cared about it. These faith-focused poems written by Pops, long before my grandson (my dad's great-grandson) was even born, have been a spiritual blessing even three generations later. Jaime, my daughter-in-love, has mentioned, "We each need to have our own book." What a joy that this has blessed her too and that she wants to carry on the tradition. Pops' faith has impacted my children, their spouses, their children, and me.

Grand Opportunities

Spontaneous conversations and planned family traditions are opportunities for us to pass along our faith and build our grandkids' faith. Being able to receive a little faith lesson from our grands also encourages their faith.

"Papa! You need to ask for forgiveness when you talk like that. Whenever I say a bad word, I stop right away and ask Jesus to forgive me." Our five-year-old grand took the position. He folded his hands, dropped his head, and prayed right then and there, "Jesus, forgive Papa for saying the "s" word (stupid). Amen."

"Thank you, you are exactly right. Thanks for praying for me. I will ask Jesus to forgive me, too."

One of the activities Papa and this grand enjoy doing together is watching silly videos on YouTube. They get a big laugh out of the funny things people do. They both love that physical humor. In this video they had watched a guy run a forklift into a stack of boxes, which tumbled down on top of him. Between laughs Tom said, "That was so stupid." Immediately our young grand acted and prayed for Papa.

Being receptive to their correction and teaching creates an atmosphere of openness, approachability, and is an additional opportunity for conversation. Allowing our grands the chance to teach us something builds their confidence and helps them embrace their faith. Scripture encourages us to be receptive to learning from our grands, "Don't let anyone look down on you because you are young, but set an example for the believers in speech, in conduct, in love, in faith and in purity" (1 Timothy 4:12).

Grand Instruction

"I get to spend time with my grandbaby almost weekly. I teach her bible stories, Bible children's songs, and I'm teaching her to pray."—Kathleen S.

Formal instruction requires more planning than off-the-cuff conversations. In 2 Timothy we find Lois, Timothy's grandmother, and Eunice, Timothy's mom, living in Lystra, a predominately Greek and godless society controlled by Rome. It is thought both Lois and Eunice' s husbands were Greek, non-believers. Nonbelieving husbands and a godless culture did not prevent Lois and Eunice from having faith and training Timothy. Paul encouraged Timothy to fan into flame the gift of God, God's gift of salvation through Jesus Christ. The faith spark created in us by God becomes a flame when we share what God has done and is doing in our lives. Our love for our grandkids fans the flame.

"God, spark a fire in my grandkids so they love and believe in Jesus. Give them the knowledge that Jesus died and rose again. Give them the understanding that sin separates them from a relationship with You and because of this forgiveness is needed. I pray they choose to serve You with the gifts and abilities You have given them. Amen."

Grand Sharing

Have you considered how you can share your faith with your grands? We have covered many direct, informal, and formal ways. Let's look at some subtle and indirect ways.

Moms Together member Sammie Walker, stay-at-home mom and worship leader, has challenged me to assess my home. Does my home speak Jesus?

Sammie says, "Music is a huge thing in our home. There is almost always worship music playing. We read the Bible every night to the kids before bed." Sammie has made an intentional decision to bring faith into every day, not just the holidays.

Look around your home and your car. Do these spaces your grandchildren enter reflect the Lord? Can my grandkids tell I love and believe in Jesus Christ? Does my home sound like Jesus? Is it filled with God-honoring music and conversation? Does my home show Jesus? What type of home décor is displayed? Do my neighborly actions give God glory? Matthew 5:16 emphasizes the importance of living a life that reflects Jesus, so through our behavior others are drawn to the Lord.

"Nana and Papa Appel had crosses hung in the hall and the kitchen. They also had a framed Serenity prayer in the hallway going into the bedroom area. I remember reading it. At first, I didn't get it but as I got older, I understood it and liked it." This prayer that Courtney read in her Nana and Papa's home years ago has impacted her life today. She says, "It puts my struggles in perspective." The Serenity prayer attributed to Reinhold Niebuhr describes how to navigate life's challenges. We need peace to accept those things that we cannot alter, have courage to adjust what is in our control, and have the ability to discern which approach is needed, acceptance or courage.

We must show and speak the Gospel. Romans 10:17 says, "faith comes from hearing the message, and the message is heard through the word about Christ." If we want to impact our grands' faith we must walk the walk, talk the talk, and talk about the walk. In Deuteronomy 4:9, God commands parents and grandparents to, "Watch yourselves closely so that you do not forget the things your eyes have seen or let them fade from your heart as long as you live. Teach them to your children and to their children after them."

Grand Telling

Where do you keep your testimony and your God stories? I tend to keep them in my head. That is not the best idea if I want these stories to outlast me. Perhaps a better approach would be to write them down. A good idea would be to keep a journal of the times God intervened, protected, blessed, or corrected me. This documentation would help me recall God-winks and then share with my grands. Depending on your story and the age of your grands you may need to apply some discretion.

I pray for God's protection and direction while I am hiking the mountain trails in Colorado. There are some places along the way where the trail is not well marked, and the GPS is not clear. Often hikers who have gone before create rock piles called cairns. These piles identify the way to go and mark significant places. This reminds me of the Ebenezer stone described in 1 Samuel 7:12. The prophet Samuel created a stone memorial to the Lord to give Him glory for the victory over their enemy the Philistines.

Create an Ebenezer memorial with your grands to celebrate and remember God's goodness. As you collect and stack flat rocks tell the story from 1 Samuel 7. Discuss God's faithful provision, protection, faithfulness, and love. Ask your grands, "When have you seen God's hand of protection, comfort, or provision?" Finish with a photo you can frame to capture the moment.

Holy encounters with the living God are meant to be recalled and celebrated. God instructed Moses to build a gold covered box, which would be filled with items that represented monumental God moments. According to Hebrews 9:4 the ark of the covenant contained Aaron's staff, the stone tablets (the ones that had the Ten Commandments on it), and a jar of manna. These items were placed inside the ark at different times. G-Mas and G-Pas, we can create something like this with our grands! It would be a faith building family activity to generate on-going conversations about significant God moments in each person's life.

Holy encounters with the living God are meant to be recalled and celebrated.

One of my first big God moments occurred when I was seven.

"It's so hot Mary Jo, let me cool you off." I assessed Mary Jo, my pet mud turtle, was getting hot in the summer sun. I grabbed a hose that was stretched out on the grass near Mary Jo. I turned on the spigot and sprayed her. The hose had been baking in the sun for hours.

"Mary Jo, Mary Jo!" Mary Jo's eyes were shut tight. I had scalded my precious turtle.

"Mom! I burned Mary Jo with the hose." Fear and dread filled my heart.

My mom came out, saw the injured turtle and her distraught daughter.

"I can't help her, but God can. Pray."

I prayed hard. I prayed with faith. I knew God could heal my turtle. Soon her eyes opened, and she crawled around. God did heal her. My faith increased.

This is a story to tell my grands. One item I could put in our family ark would be a toy turtle.

Let's take time to discuss our personal relationship and interactions with the Creator of the universe. It gives our grand's a glimpse into our lives and relationship with the Lord.

The least complicated way to build a family ark of the covenant, would be to paint or wrap a box. I'm not very creative so it may stop there with me but for those of you who are more creative, check out the description of the ark in Exodus 25:10–22 and have at it!

God understood the value of memorials, so He instructed Joshua to collect stones out of the Jordan riverbed. "And Joshua set up at Gilgal the twelve stones they had taken out of the Jordan. He said to the Israelites, "In the future when your descendants ask their parents, 'What do these stones mean?' tell them, 'Israel crossed the Jordan on dry ground'" (Joshua 4:20–22).

Grand Uniqueness

Just as the Lord has a unique relationship with each of us, we will have a special relationship with each of our grands. It is in that uniqueness we can strengthen our relationship. With one of my granddaughters, I speak with an English accent and call her, "Ma'Lady." One day when I arrived at her home, I was removing my shoes by the front door. She flung her arms out and declared in a Town Cryer way, "I have an announcement to make, Ma'Lady is here."

She loves pretending. Sometimes she's Ma'Lady and other times she is the Doctor. (The Doctor can get a little bossy.) Fellow Nonas and Pappies, we can strengthen our relationship as we notice each grand's unique gifting, personality, and interests. One of my grandkids is fascinated by Tardigrades. I have to say, he is teaching me a lot about these eight-legged microscopic arthropods. Another grand is captivated by Sea Dragons. Look them up along with Tardigrades. They are a real thing! Sort of like a Sea Horse but even cooler and much larger.

Nature is one of God's best ways to draw us to Himself. Take the opportunity to find "the thing" and then bring God as Creator into the conversation.

Grand Style

Grandparents, we are unique too. We bring our own gifts and personality to the table. Just as we were created to be our children's parents, we are also fashioned to be our grandkids' grandparents. Our grands need what we have to offer. If we can combine the best of our grandparenting style with the Christian Coach, we are off to a powerful start to make a positive difference in our grandchildren's spiritual life and development.

Our unique efforts, if exerted in the spirit of family love, unity, interdependency, humility, and respect will have a big and positive impact on our grand's lives today and in eternity.

As I was working on this chapter, Tom received a phone call that one of his employees had passed away the night before. There were no warning signs. His wife is in complete shock. This surprising and sad event reminded me of what Scripture tells us about our lives. Our days are numbered.

God has set eternity in our hearts. We want our children and their children and their children's children to join us in eternity. Let's partner with our adult children and with God to influence and impact our grands life today and eternity to come. It is my heart, and I think yours too, for my grands to love Jesus, know Jesus, serve Jesus, and meet me in Heaven with Jesus. This is the best gift of all. Psalm 90:12 wisely states, "Teach us to number our days, that we may gain a heart of wisdom."

Grand Command

We were born for such a time as this. So were your children and grandchildren. Have no fear, have faith. Be like Joshua and Caleb (Numbers 13–14), who trusted God with next steps. We have a charge from our Great God to walk out in God-confidence and battle alongside the Lord for our grandkids' faith.

I will open my mouth with a parable; I will utter hidden things, things from of old—things we have heard and known, things our ancestors have told us. We will not hide them from their descendants; we will tell the next generation the praiseworthy deeds of the Lord, his power, and the wonders he has done. He decreed statutes for Jacob and established the law in Israel, which he commanded our ancestors to teach their children, so the next generation would know them even the children yet to be born, and they in turn would tell their children. Then they would put their trust in God and would not forget his deeds but would keep his commands.

Psalm 78:2–7

Grand Reflection

1. What type of conversations do you have with your grandkids? How can you weave faith into those times?
2. Which idea presented in this chapter are you likely to implement?
3. Decide how and when you will tell your grandkids your faith story.

Grand Verses

Read, reflect, and respond to these verses:

- Job 7:7

- Psalm 102:3
- James 4:14
- Revelation 20:15
- 2 Corinthians 4:18
- 2 Corinthians 5:1–10
- Exodus 20:5–6

What do you learn from these passages?

Grand Partner Tips

- Take time to study Scripture so you are ready to answer your grand's questions.
- If you do not know the answer, learn the answer with your grand.
- Include formal and informal faith-filled interactions in the time you are with your grands.

Grand Prayer

Lord God,

Thank you for the blessing of grandchildren. Use me to support my adult children to build my grandkids relationship with You. Amen.

Grand Parent Charge

Go and be the grandparent God has called
you to be for such a time as this.

"My life is blessed; I have held my children's children."
—Jeremy Taylor

Suggested Grandparent Resources

Grand Monday Nights Weekly Webinar

A free weekly webinar about Intentional Christian Grandparenting with new and relevant topics and speakers each week hosted by Barb Lorenz with Patsy Glunt or Lori Wildenberg as guest hosts. This webinar is produced by Larry Fowler's Legacy Coalition. https://legacycoalition.com/grand-monday-nights/.

The Legacy Coalition

Provides help for grandparents to have a greater spiritual impact on their families through the weekly webinar (Grand Monday Nights), Grandparenting Matters Seminars, Grandparent Summit National Conferences. https://legacycoalition.com/.

Online Resources

Biblicalparenting.org

CelebrateKids.com

FamTime.com

GrandkidsMatter.org

LoriWildenberg.com

Moms Together Facebook group and community page

RaisingChristianKids.com/tips-from-the-experts/

Visionaryfam.com

Podcasts

D6 Family Ministry Podcast

Moms Together, Moms Better Together, Raising Christian Kids—MOMents with Lori and Lee Ann

Lori's YouTube Channel https://www.youtube.com/c/Lori-Wildenberg

Eryn Lynum's *Rooted in Wonder* podcast

Print Resources

Becky Danielson and Carol Olsen, *Faithful Grandparenting: Practical Ideas for Connecting the Generations*

Ken Canfield, *The H.E.A.R.T of Grandparenting: 5 Keys to Being the Best Grandparent Possible*

Larry Fowler, *Overcoming Grandparenting Barriers: How to Navigate Painful Problems With Grace and Truth*

Cavin Harper, *Courageous Grandparenting: Unshakable Faith in a Broken World*

Kathy Koch, *Resilient Kids: Raising Them to Embrace Life With Confidence*

Eryn Lynum, *Rooted in Wonder: Nurturing Your Family's Faith Through God's Creation*

Lee Ann Mancini, *Raising Kids to Follow Christ: Instilling a Lifelong Trust in God*

Larry E. McCall, *Grandparenting With Grace: Living the Gospel With the Next Generation*

Josh Mulvihill, *Grand Parenting: Strengthening Your Family and Passing Along Your Faith*

Wayne Rice, *Long Distance Grandparenting: Nurturing the Faith of Your Grandchildren When You Can't Be There in Person*

Christie Thomas, *Little Habits, Big Faith: How Simple Practices Help Your Family Grow in Jesus*

Scott Turansky, *Grandparenting With Purpose: Opening the Windows of Influence*

Lori Wildenberg, *The Messy Life of Parenting: Powerful and Practical Ways to Strengthen Family Connections*

Lori Wildenberg, *Messy Hope: Help Your Child Overcome Anxiety, Depression, or Suicidal Ideation*

Lori Wildenberg, *Messy Journey: How Grace and Truth Offer the Prodigal a Way Home*

About the Author

Helping families build connections that last a lifetime is Lori Wildenberg's passion. She has over thirty years of experience working with families to help them be who God created them to be.

Professionally, Lori is a licensed parent and family educator, national speaker, co-founder of 1 Corinthians 13 Parenting Ministry, owner and lead mentor for the Moms Together Community and Group found on Facebook, and author or co-author of seven parenting or grandparenting books. Lori is a member of the Advanced Writers and Speakers Association. You can find articles by Lori at *Focus on the Family, Mom Life Today, Just Between Us, Crosswalk,* and other online Christian magazines.

Personally, Lori is wife to Tom, her college sweetheart, and mom of four. The Wildenberg family has experienced a growth spurt with a daughter-in-love, two sons-in-love, and five grands. A perfect day in Lori's world is a hike with any combination of family members and of course Toby the family goldendoodle. The Wildenberg home is nestled in the foothills of the Rocky Mountains. For more information, to connect with, or to receive Lori's quarterly newsletter go to loriwildenberg.com.

Endnotes

1 "Study: Middle Age Across America," *Mixbook*, May 23, 2023, https://www.mixbook.com/inspiration/study-middle-age-across-america, (accessed January 15, 2025).

2 Fast Facts on Grandparenting & Intergenerational Mentoring," *Legacy Project.Org,* https://www.legacyproject.org/specialreports/fastfacts.html (accessed June 14, 2024).

3 Ibid.

4 Ibid.

5 "How Caring for Grandchildren Can Boost Your Health," *Henry Ford Health Staff*, (October 19, 2023), https://www.henryford.com/blog/2023/10/how-caring-for-grandchildren-can-boost-your-health (accessed January 11, 2025).

6 Ibid.

7 "Fast Facts on Grandparenting & Intergenerational Mentoring," *Legacy Project.Org,* https://www.legacyproject.org/specialreports/fastfacts.html (accessed June 14, 2024).

8 Kaitlyn Phoenix, "Scientists Say Grandparents Can Have a Big Impact on a Mom's Mental Health," *Good Housekeeping,* March 9, 2024, https://www.goodhousekeeping.com/health/wellness/a46935174/grandparents-support-mother-mental-health/ (accessed January 11, 2025).

9 Josh Mulvihill, *Discipling Your Grandchildren: Great Ideas to Help Them Know, Love, and Serve God,* (Bloomington: Bethany House, 2020), 31.

10 Moradeke Owa, "The Goldilocks Principle: What It Is and How to Apply It," *Formplus,* Updated January 17, 2025, https://www.formpl.us/blog/the-goldilocks-principle-what-it-is-how-to-apply-it.

11 Fast Facts on Grandparenting and Intergenerational Mentoring, *The Legacy Project* https://www.legacyproject.org/specialreports/fastfacts.html (accessed January 10, 2025).

12 Ibid.

13 Cavin Harper, *Courageous Grandparenting: Unshakeable Faith in a Broken World*, (Colorado Springs: The Christian Grandparenting Network, 2013), 35.

14 Larry Fowler, Grandparent Workshop, Grace Church of Arvada, Arvada, CO, January 27, 2024.

15 "Grandparents: A Critical Child Care Safety Net," *National Association of Child Care Resource & Referral Agencies*, https://www.childcareaware.org/wp-content/uploads/2015/10/2008_grandparents_report-finalrept.pdf, vi, (accessed June 3, 2024).

16 Diane Fowler, conversation with Diane at the Grandparent Workshop at Grace Church in Arvada, CO, (January 24, 2024).

17 Jaycee Dunn, "What to Do About Uninvolved Grandparents," *Parents* magazine (May 2023, Updated October 30, 2024). https://www.parents.com/parenting/dynamics/grandparents/uninvolved-grandparents/.

18 Homer Simpson, *The Simpsons*, You Tube video (0.0-0.4). https://www.youtube.com/watch?v=H6CLCiRBUP0.

19 John Ortberg, *Everybody's Normal Till You Get to Know Them* (Grand Rapids: Zondervan, 2014).

20 Lori Wildenberg, *The Messy Life of Parenting: Powerful and Practical Ways to Strengthen Family Connections* (Birmingham: Iron Stream Media, 2018), 17.

21 Ibid., 10–13.

22 Fowler, Grandparent Workshop.

23 Larry Fowler, *Overcoming Grandparenting Barriers: How to Navigate Painful Problems With Grace and Truth* (Minneapolis: Bethany House, 2009), 72–73.

24 Ibid.

25 Larry Fowler, Grandparenting Matters seminar, Grace Church Arvada, January 27, 2024.

26 Brooke Auxier, Monica Anderson, Andrew Perrin and Erica Turner, "Parenting Children in the Age of Screens," *Pew Research Center*, July 28, 2020, https://www.pewresearch.org/internet/2020/07/28/parenting-children-in-the-age-of-screens/, (accessed October 15, 2024).

[27] "How to Cope With Family Estrangement," *Gransnet Daily*, https://www.gransnet.com/grandparenting/how-to-cope-with-estrangement, (accessed January 11, 2025).

[28] "In U.S. Decline of Christianity Continues at Rapid Pace," *Pew Research*, October 17, 2019, https://www.pewresearch.org/religion/2019/10/17/in-u-s-decline-of-christianity-continues-at-rapid-pace/ (accessed January 12, 2025).

[29] Ibid.

[30] Ryan P. Burge, "Gen Z and Religion in 2022," *Religion in Public*, https://religioninpublic.blog/2023/04/03/gen-z-and-religion-in-2022/, (accessed January 12, 2025).

[31] Daniel A. Cox, "Generation Z and the Future of Faith in America," *Survey Center on American Life,* March 24, 2022, https://www.americansurveycenter.org/research/generation-z-future-of-faith/, (accessed January 12, 2025).

[32] "What Does It Mean for a Society to Be Post-Christian?" *Got Questions*, https://www.gotquestions.org/post-Christian.html, (accessed October 19, 2024).

[33] Larry Fowler, *Overcoming Grandparenting Barriers*, 83.

[34] Joshua Coleman, *Rules of Estrangement: Why Adult Children Cut Ties and How to Heal the Conflict* (New York: Harmony Books, 2020), 33.

[35] Lucy Blake, "Why Men's Relationships Are More Fragile," *Psychology Today*, November 21, 2022, https://www.psychologytoday.com/us/blog/real-families/202211/why-mens-family-relationships-are-more-fragile, (accessed October 21, 2024).

[36] Ibid.

[37] Wildenberg, *The Messy Life of Parenting*, 10.

[38] Ibid, 13.

[39] Lee Bare, "Why Should Your Son Hear You Say You are Proud of Him?" *Psychology Today*, posted April 20, 2020. https://www.psychologytoday.com/us/blog/boys-will-be-boys/202004/why-should-your-son-hear-you-say-you-are-proud-of-him, (accessed January 12, 2025).

[40] Charles Haddon Spurgeon, *The Power of Prayer in a Believer's Life*, ed. Robert Hall (Seattle: YWAM, 1996).

41 Charles Haddon Spurgeon, "My Times Are in Thy Hand," Sunday Sermon, May 17,1891.

42 Jeff Wallenfeldt, "7 (or 8) Summits: The World's Highest Mountains by Continent," *Britannica*, https://www.britannica.com/story/7-or-8-summits-the-worlds-highest-mountains-by-continent (accessed December 30, 2024).

43 Ibid.

44 Elizabeth Spencer, "Prayer for a New Year," *No Greater Joy* Facebook posted December 31, 2024, (accessed December 31, 2024).

45 David Kithcart, "St. Valentine, the Real Story," CBN The Christian Broadcast Network, https://cbn.com/article/valentines-day/st-valentine-real-story, (accessed January 2, 2025).

46 Ibid.

47 "St. Patrick," *Biography*, https://www.biography.com/religious-figures/saint-patrick, Updated March 14, 2023.

48 Lori Wildenberg, "How to Create a Faith and Fun Filled Easter Basket," *Eternal Moments* blog, https://loriwildenberg.com/2024/03/19/how-to-create-a-faith-and-fun-filled-easter-basket/ updated March 19, 2024, (accessed January 2, 2025).

49 "A Long, Cold Road to Bethlehem: Nativity: Gospel Accounts of Mary and Joseph's Journey Gloss Over the Arduous Reality of Life and Travel in Ancient Galilee," *Los Angeles Times Archives*, December 23, 1995, https://www.latimes.com/archives/la-xpm-1995-12-23-me-17102-story.html, (accessed January 2, 2025).